Forging a Human Future

ALSO BY ERIKA ERDMANN

Realism and Human Values (1978)

Challenge to Humanity: Values for Survival and Progress (1989)

Beyond a World Divided: Human Values in the Mind-Brain Science of Roger W. Sperry (1991)
(with David Stover)

A Mind for Tomorrow: Facts, Values, and the Future (2000)
(with David Stover)

FORGING A HUMAN FUTURE

Erika Erdmann

Edited, and with an Introduction and Notes, by David Stover

A New Road Book

Rock's Mills Press

2012

A New Road Book

PUBLISHED BY
Rock's Mills Press
2645 Castle Hill Crescent
Oakville, Ontario, Canada
L6H 6J1

First Edition

Contents

Preface

Why a collection of writings by Erika Erdmann? For that matter, who *was* Erika Erdmann?

Good questions, both. Erika Erdmann is not a household name. Yet if civilization survives the many challenges facing it in the twenty-first century, some small measure of the credit should go to her. For after a life already fuller than most, she devoted her final three decades to finding humane solutions to the problems of the human future. Networking with Nobel laureates, immersing herself in the intricacies of neuroscience, writing books and magazine articles, maintaining a lively correspondence with hundreds of like-minded thinkers the world over, Erika Erdmann believed passionately that only by finding common ground among science, ethics, and religion could a human future be forged.

Though Erika Erdmann is not a household name, many of her friends, correspondents, and co-workers were (and are) well known: Roger Sperry, the Nobel Prize-winning psychologist famous for his split-brain research; Robert Muller, assistant secretary general of the United Nations; Ervin Laszlo, philosopher of science and futurist; and K. Eric Drexler, prophet of the nanotechnology revolution. Like them, Erdmann was seized with deep concern for what the future would bring. Only by embracing new ways of thinking and acting in the world, she believed, could humanity successfully navigate the troubled waters ahead. Yet unlike many futurists, Erdmann grounded her views in common sense and everyday reality. Though she did not believe in the traditional Christian view of God as an omnipotent supernatural being, she was deeply aware of the meaning and resonance that religious beliefs bring to people's lives. And while she enjoyed a considerable knowledge of science and the scientific method, and deplored the attempts by many New Age thinkers to discard science's hard-won triumphs, she nonetheless believed that a true understanding of science left ample room in the world for human values, emotions, and ideals. Indeed, such qualities, far from being eliminated from the world by science, were, in Erdmann's view, validated by it: human consciousness is a naturally occurring, emergent property of the highly complex matter that makes up the human brain. We ignore its reality at our peril.

In the pages that follow, I have gathered together Erdmann's most important writings from her books, numerous journal articles, and more than five dozen issues of the journal, *Humankind Advancing,* that she published quarterly. As an introductory essay, I have also included my own biographical memoir of this remarkable individual.

At the core of Erdmann's world view were the complementary concepts of *emergence* and *downward causation.* The opening selections of the book explain these concepts, which serve as the linchpin tying together science and human values. Subsequent essays elaborate on the nature of that linkage and why it is so important, as well as discussing in detail the contributions of Roger Sperry to the contemporary understanding of human consciousness. In the final chapters, Erdmann considers the problems confronting civilization in light of such ideas. The collection closes with several pieces that are more personal, including the moving "Letter to a Sister," which in many ways sums up Erdmann's lifework.

It was my great privilege to count Erika Erdmann a friend for more than a quarter of a century. Seldom are such keen intelligence and goodness of heart so well matched. In our media-mad world, fame is all too often given to those who least merit it, while the deserving labor in obscurity. I hope this collection will help keep Erika Erdmann's thoughts and ideals alive for new generations of readers and thinkers.

DAVID STOVER
Oakville, Ontario

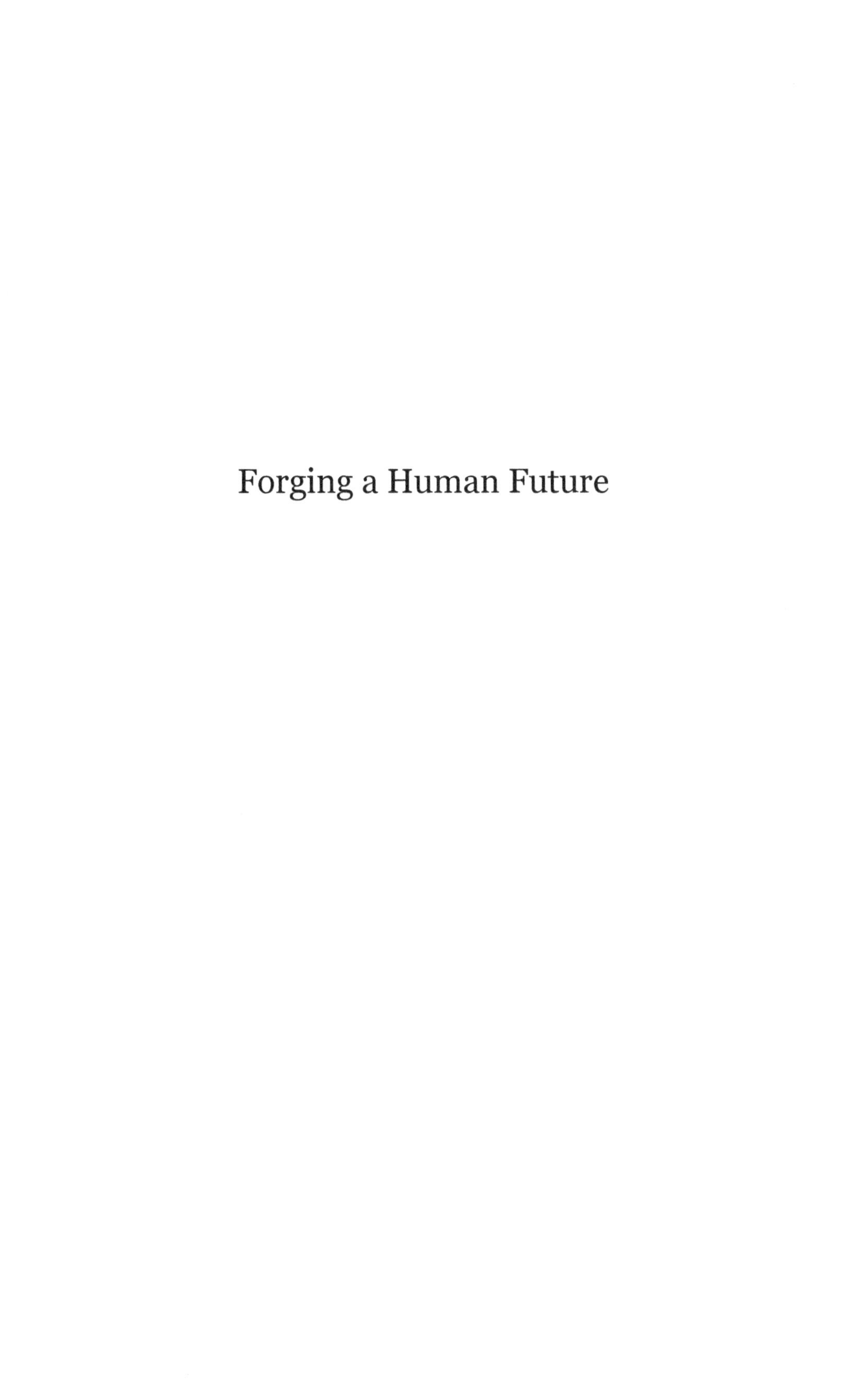

Forging a Human Future

CHAPTER ONE

Into the Future

A Biographical Memoir by David Stover

Though I corresponded with her for a quarter of a century, collaborated on two books, and counted her among my oldest and closest friends, I met Erika Erdmann only once. That was at an academic conference, and the woman I met there was a curious combination of frailty and strength: thin, small-boned, skin pulled tightly across her cheekbones, almost birdlike in her rapid movements. Yet at the same time she gave off a tremendous sense of determination and intellectual vitality. Her eyes always seemed to be measuring, evaluating, assessing. Though by that point in her life she was already a grandmother several times over, there was little softness there, beneath the horn-rimmed glasses and the hair pulled back in a tight bun. And her thick German accent—she often reversed the usual English order of subject and verb—lent a final intimidating touch.

Talking to Erdmann, in person or on the phone, it sometimes seemed as though ideas flooded out more quickly than words or phrases could be found to frame them. That might have had something to do with the fact that English was her second language, learned only as an adult. But the more important reason, I suspect, was that Erdmann was a woman in a hurry. Only in her sixties did she have the opportunity to begin her life's work, and when she did she chose a project of no mean scope—popularizing ideas that she believed were essential to the very survival of civilization.

The dichotomy between science and religion—reason and faith—runs deep in the Western intellectual tradition. At some fundamental level it hints of an even more profound divide in the human spirit, that chasm between the world as it is and the world as we would like it to be that opens in childhood and widens inexorably thereafter. As such, it runs like a thread through all of our lives, expressed in numberless and various ways, whether in the poignancy of unrequited love or the quiet melancholy one feels in the presence of a perfect sunset and the accompanying realization that a moment once fled will never come again.

For much of her life, Erika Erdmann was preoccupied with the nature of this divide and its implications for the human future. Perhaps that was not surprising, given her background. Born in Germany, she was barely a teenager when Hitler came to power. She witnessed firsthand the corrosive effects of a new and toxic mixture of populism and racial hatred on the institutions of one of the most scientifically and culturally advanced nations in the world. The optimistic assumption of the Victorians that technological and humanitarian progress could and would march hand in hand had been fatally undercut by the cataclysm of the First World War and the ensuing chaos of the post-war world. But the rise of Nazism with its peculiarly successful blend of the atavistic and the ultra-modern—torchlight parades and ballistic missiles—seemed to foreshadow a future in which science, far from liberating humanity through the advance of knowledge, would instead serve as a new and terrible instrument of fear and oppression, appealing to the deepest, darkest instincts of the human psyche.

More than one historian has remarked on the strangely schizophrenic nature of the twentieth century. The century's first half was dominated by the rise of fascism and communism, by economic disruption and downturn, by mass genocide, and by the most terrible wars humanity had ever experienced, vast globe-encircling conflicts in which tens of millions perished. By contrast, the century's second half, though darkened by the shadows of the Cold War and the looming specter of thermonuclear doom, brought with it for hundreds of millions of people fortunate enough to be living in the so-called "First World" nations of the West a period of unprecedented economic well-being, social progress, and technological advancement. It was as if after the last bone-jarring thunderclaps of Hiroshima and Nagasaki, the terrible storm clouds had parted and the sun reappeared.

Erdmann's life followed something of the same arc. Caught up in the vast wave of refugee migrations that swept eastern and central Europe in the immediate aftermath of World War II, she and her family emigrated to Canada in 1953. There they proceeded to build a comfortable middle-class existence no different than that enjoyed by millions of other Canadians and Americans of the period, she and her husband Karl raising their four children while he moved forward in his engineering career.

Not until she reached her late 40s did the scientific and philosophical concerns of her youth in Germany reassert themselves. After completing a degree in psychology at Montreal's Sir George Williams University (now Concordia University), Erdmann became increasingly interested in the work of Roger W. Sperry, the American neuroscientist who had first come to prominence in the early 1960s for his so-called "split brain" work. Sperry's research on the nature of the brain's left and right hemispheres generated important insights into how the brain was structured. It also led to a widely held but grievously oversimplified view (one Sperry did not share) of the brain's being divided into a left hemisphere that was the seat of rational, logical thought and a right hemisphere that served as the center of intuitive, holistic patterns of thought. As with many oversimplifications, there was a germ of truth at the bottom of it. The two cerebral hemispheres *do* function in significantly different ways, and to a surprising degree the dichotomy between rationality and emotion I spoke of earlier is embodied in the structure and operation of the brain itself. Nor can Sperry and his co-workers be blamed for the overzealous response to their ideas that gave birth to a whole genre of popularizations with titles like *Drawing on the Righthand Side of the Brain*. For that matter, one suspects the popular enthusiasm engendered by Sperry's rather recondite reports on the effects of severing the bundle of nerve fibers linking the two hemispheres reflected a growing cultural concern with the differences between the radically different ways of approaching the world represented by what might, at their broadest, be termed "thinking" and "feeling."

These were the Sixties, after all—the era both of technocracy's greatest accomplishment, the moon landing, and the widespread renunciation of technocratic, rationalistic values that was represented by the youth counter-culture and the anti-war movement. Small wonder that a suggestion these conflicting viewpoints might be hardwired into the species found a ready reception. . . .

Sperry's view was always more subtle. Though the split-brain work represented the apex of his scientific career and would earn him a share in the Nobel Prize in medicine and physiology not quite two decades later, by the late 1960s he had moved on to consider the broader question of the nature of human consciousness and what it had to say about the relationship of science and religion in general. Sperry was scarcely alone in pursuing such interests. C.P. Snow had made the entire question of the relationship between science and the humanities practically a household word with the publication of his famous polemic on *The Two Cultures* in 1960; and Jacob Bronowski, a mathematician who wrote widely on both science and the humanities, including a well-regarded monograph on the poetry of William Blake, attempted what is perhaps still our time's preeminent attempt at a popular synthesis of scientific and humanistic ways of thinking with his famous 1972 BBC television series, *The Ascent of Man*.

Sperry's own work in this area never commanded the same attention as that of Snow or Bronowski, but it was in some regards even more ambitious. In a series of scientific and philosophical papers that began to appear in the mid-1960s, Sperry argued that consciousness is an "emergent property" of the physiochemical functioning of the brain. As such, consciousness is utterly dependent on the brain's physical existence—there is no such thing as a disembodied soul or spirit that can exist apart from the physical brain or survive its demise—but at the same time it cannot be reduced merely to the sum of the brain's physical processes. The whole is more than the sum of its parts: consciousness emerges from the workings of the brain and, because it exists at a higher level of organization, coordinates and controls those workings in the same way that values—systems of ethical priorities and moral precepts—emerge from the more mundane facts of the physical and social world and help humans give order and priority to those facts. The dichotomy between facts and values, between science and religion, is, at its roots, a false one. Facts and values alike are part of a coherent sequence of mental constructions of ever-increasing abstraction and complexity that influence and inform each other. The facts of the material world helped form human values in the first place, and such values are just as much adaptations evolved to further an individual's or species' chances of survival in that world as the protective coloration of the zebra or the vicious teeth of the tyrannosaur. At the same time, employed by a species with (so far as we know) the unique gift of reason and abstraction, such values help humanity decide which material facts are important and how we should act on them.

Sperry's view, then, was of an integrated realm of knowledge in which scientific fact helped inform value judgments and, in turn, ethical considerations directed and gave meaning to scientific inquiry. And even as the much-lauded neuroscientist was laying out his argument in paper after closely-reasoned paper, an obscure part-time librarian was struggling toward the same conclusions.

It was in 1972, following her husband Karl's retirement, that Erdmann had settled in southwestern Nova Scotia, near the village of Lockeport. There she and Karl lived for more than a quarter-century, in a house overlooking the moss-covered rocks and surging spray of the North Atlantic coastline. Erdmann soon began working as a part-time assistant for the local library system, and it was during this time that, building on both her undergraduate work in psychology and on the experiences of a long and varied life, she began to draw together her ideas about how science could be used to improve humanity's lot rather than degrade it. In 1978, she paid a New York-based vanity press to publish those ideas in a slim volume entitled *Realism and Human Values*.

The book is not an easy read, something Erdmann herself recognized: "This book contains all the flaws of the work of a single person who did not know anyone with whom to talk the subject matter over . . . There was simply nobody [of whom] to ask questions." That being said, it is a remarkably concise treatment of a theme Erdmann was to develop in greater detail over the course of the next two decades, both working with Sperry and on her own, a theme summed up in the book's epigraph: *Mutual concern and objective knowledge are interdependent*. There, in seven words, lay the nucleus of her life's work: a profound conviction (and equally profound need to tell the world of that conviction) that the worlds of thinking and feeling were not irrevocably opposed; that, in fact, unless those two sides of the human character could find a constructive way of working together, all might be lost. Mankind might survive, but at the cost of its humanity. The choice was set out starkly on the very first page:

> Three ways into the future are open to us. First, the human species or even all life on earth will cease to be; second, man continues to live in the form of a highly intelligent and efficient animal while humanity is destroyed; third, man and his humanity survive. The present book has been written to initiate thoughts and discussions that increase the probability of the third way into the future.

Erdmann went on to argue that such a dichotomy was—however compelling it might seem on first glance—erroneous; and that a truly comprehensive view of the "real" world encompassed both objective knowledge *and* human values. In short, she believed it was high time for concerned individuals to come to the defense of realism, before the opposing forces of the two cultures conspired in a mutually assured destruction of their own that might hold consequences for humanity different but just as dire as those threatened by global thermonuclear war.

It was a thought-provoking thesis, but Erdmann soon discovered that she had chosen the wrong vehicle to disseminate her ideas. Books put out by vanity presses aren't reviewed, aren't stocked by bookstores or purchased by libraries, aren't taken seriously; and in those pre-Internet days of 1978 no cost-effective way existed for an independent researcher and writer of modest means to publicize her work. No more than a few dozen copies of *Realism and Human Values* were ever distributed. But

Erdmann used the book as a springboard back into academe: in 1981, at the age of 62, she began graduate work under Kraft von Maltzahn in the biology department at Dalhousie University in Halifax, Nova Scotia, concentrating on the integration of science and values, with a special focus on the contributions of Roger Sperry and Ralph Burhoe, a pioneer in the study of the relationship between science and religion. She had also taken the bold step of sending a copy of *Realism and Human Values* to Roger Sperry himself; and, somewhat to her surprise—for Nobel prizewinners are besieged by unsolicited mail and manuscripts—he read the book, saw in her a kindred spirit, and invited her to come to Pasadena to work for him as a research assistant at the California Institute of Technology. "The chances are less than one in a million," he told the Immigration and Naturalization Service when Erdmann applied for a visa, "that I could ever find anyone else so knowledgeable . . . and deeply motivated to assist me in this very specialized area." *Realism and Human Values* had done its work. Erdmann requested a leave of absence from her studies at Dalhousie to go to Pasadena. Late in life, Erika Erdmann was able to embark wholeheartedly on her life's work.

Erdmann spent nearly a decade working with Sperry. She and Karl in effect commuted from Nova Scotia to California, spending the winters in Pasadena, returning to their beloved home by the sea in Nova Scotia for the summer. Her years as Sperry's library assistant were both enormously rewarding yet incredibly frustrating. Though a giant of twentieth-century neuroscience and a supremely gifted experimentalist and theorist, Sperry could also be a difficult person to work for and with—demanding, sometimes cantankerous, and a perfectionist both in regard to his own work and that of others. The fact that late in life Sperry suffered from a degenerative neurological disorder no doubt heightened his sense that time was running out and hence his impatience with work he viewed as inadequate or incomplete.

Nonetheless, Erdmann found her close association with Sperry and the circle of graduate students and researchers surrounding him at Caltech intensely stimulating. She even found time to carry out research of her own. Unconcerned at this point in her life with academic prestige but eager to explore the links between science and human values with the maximum degree of latitude possible, she completed first a master's degree and then a doctorate through the California distance education institution Columbia Pacific University, under the supervision of psychologist Frank Cardelle. Although Columbia Pacific was to become notorious in the 1990s as an unaccredited "degree mill" that failed to meet state regulatory standards and was ultimately closed down by court order, Erdmann's research was exactly the kind of untraditional, cross-disciplinary effort that would have been hard-pressed to find a home elsewhere.

Her master's thesis, "In Search of a Unifying World View," served as the basis for the book, *Beyond a World Divided: Human Values in the Brain-Mind Science of Roger Sperry,* which I co-authored with her and which was published by Shambhala in 1990. Her work revising the manuscript was carried out in close collaboration with Sperry, a process she no doubt found both useful—if you're going to write a book about someone's scientific and philosophical worldview, it's a tremendous help to have the subject of the book close at hand to discuss his ideas—but also intimidating, given Sperry's incessant need to critique, revise, and redraft not only his own work but that of others. Her own epilogue to the book, included in this collection, provides a poignant yet unvarnished portrait of the man who had exerted such an enormous influence on her own life.

Even while working on the manuscript that would become *Beyond a World Divided,* Erdmann was finishing her doctoral dissertation. Though Columbia Pacific was criticized for granting doctorates on the basis of dissertations that were only a few dozen pages long and lacked any measure of quantitative or analytical rigor, Erdmann's dissertation, "In Search of Values for Human Survival," is legitimate, if unorthodox, academic work that employed the ideas of thinkers such as Sperry and Burhoe as a jumping-off point for a deeper exploration of the values animating North American society in general and, in particular, that society's response to global problems such as overpopulation, resource depletion, and economic inequality. Erdmann carried out her research under the supervision of Cardelle and of Hanna and Alan Newcombe of the Peace Research Institute—Dundas, a Canadian non-profit organization based near Hamilton, Ontario devoted to the furthering of academic work in the areas of peace studies, international relations, and disarmament. Erdmann sent questionnaires to 716 individuals, leaders (in her words) in "ten different sectors of North American society (religion, philosophy, science, humanities, mass media, promoters of science-religion interaction, peace, a sustainable society, technological progress, and 'other concerned persons')." She received 221 replies, which she then analyzed both quantitatively and qualitatively, concluding that, although a majority of respondents espoused the same underlying aims and values, their recommendations for action often differed enormously, because of individuals' backgrounds, education, philosophical views, and experiences. Saving the planet, Erdmann concluded, wasn't as easy as merely getting everyone to agree it *should* be saved: "Lethal tensions may still occur—even if the question of values is solved—unless the factor of background assumptions is considered." Indeed, she singled out the project's most important finding as

> the discovery that even if aims are identical, and even if values are identical, suggestions for actions to be taken may be vastly different, depending on a respondent's background and personal experiences. –Therefore, not values themselves, but the perception of reality from which they arise and through which they are interpreted and translated into action, must demand our main attention.

All the same, her research showed some basis for common ground. While most of those who responded to her survey could not accept a system of ethics based solely on science, they "would accept a world view which integrates man and nature, mind and matter, science and values." The biggest problem, of course, was how to devise such a world view—and how to ensure it achieved widespread acceptance. It is probably unfair to burden a research study on values necessary for survival with the even more enormous task of translating those values into action. But Erdmann did make some tentative suggestions which, if clearly inadequate to the task at hand, nonetheless represent a step in the right direction. Perhaps the most concrete was the idea of creating private foundations which, freed from the imperatives of commercial success, could disseminate ideas and theories meant to encourage a more future-oriented, responsible way of addressing society's challenges.

Inspiration for that suggestion may have come in part from the example of the Newcombes themselves and their institute, which had played such a major role in encouraging the growth of peace studies as an academic discipline. In fact, a condensed version of Erdmann's dissertation was published in the March 1989 issue of the Institute's *Peace Research Reviews* under the title "Challenge to Humanity: Values for Survival and Progress." Such publication brought Erdmann's research to a wider audience, for which she was grateful—as she noted in her foreword, no less than 84 academic institutions had turned down her idea for a research project on the values needed for human survival before the Newcombes and Columbia Pacific provided a home for such work. At the same time, Erdmann's views were not entirely in the mainstream of the peace studies movement. She remained skeptical of claims that unilateral disarmament would augur in an era of universal peace, in her dissertation declaring:

> We need peace. But peace cannot be achieved through relinquishment of weapons before sufficient mental maturity worldwide has been established to rely on contracts and just laws. Unilateral disarmament at the present time would not secure peace; it might increase hatred and cruelty through the silencing of voices of reason. Even dominance of [a] worldwide totalitarian regime would not bring peace, nor would it guarantee the survival of humanity. Through the ruthless combat of internal dissent and passionate reaction to it, more frightening and easily hidden weapons, such as chemical or biological ones, might be developed.

No doubt the experiences of Erdmann and her family, first in Nazi Germany and then, after the Second World War, in a Soviet-run refugee camp, loomed large in her mind as she wrote those words. As Russian troops closed in on the German capital, Erdmann fled through enemy lines with her two children, one two-and-a-half years old, the other only four months. Failing to reach asylum in the west, she was shot in the leg by a Russian soldier; the bullet left an exit wound the size of a person's palm. Thousands of injured and dying German soldiers filled the camp where she and her family were interned. During the long nights she lay awake listening to the sounds of a nearby train station, where German POWs were loaded into freight cars for the long ride to Siberian labor camps. A prisoner who somehow escaped told her that the cars were completely sealed, all windows and other openings nailed shut. Only by gouging out breathing holes in the floors of the cars could the unwilling passengers stave off suffocation. Clearly nuclear weapons were not the only manifestation of man's inhumanity to man, or the sole threat to civilization's survival.

By 1990 Erdmann found her work with Sperry increasingly stressful. His relentless demands for perfection were part of the problem, as were philosophical differences between the two. Sperry, like most biologists of his generation, saw competition as the engine driving evolution forward. If science were to shape a better future, the key role played by competition in improving species—including our own—must be recognized. Sperry might not accept the Victorian definition of evolution as the product of "nature red in tooth and claw." But he surely would have espoused the view popularized by health clubs and manufacturers of exercise equipment: No pain, no gain. For Sperry, competition was vital to humanity's advancement, and a certain amount of suffering was inevitable as the strong prosper and the weak fall by the wayside.

Erdmann, on the other hand, saw a greater role for cooperation in advancing humanity toward a better future. Instances of cooperation among individuals of the same species, or even between individuals from different species, are more common than had once been thought. And, in Erdmann's view, many if not most advances in human civilization came through the ability of people to put individual differences aside and cooperate in the service of a greater good.

Then, too, age played a role: she was 71 now, and eager to spend her remaining years close to her beloved Atlantic coast. But she wasn't ready to stop working. Instead, she threw her energies into a new outlet: a self-published quarterly journal, highlighting developments in the study of science, values, and global problems. She called the journal *Humankind Advancing,* and its statement of purpose declared:

> Our progress through evolution and history at the present time has been compared with the passage of a water craft through the foaming, boiling waters of a canyon. Rocks and boulders, partly visible and partly submerged, produce dangerous whirlpools and call for the utmost skill and vigilance of the pilot. —I see the rocks as dogmas, the whirlpools as illusions, and humankind in desperate need of capable pilots. The aim of the present periodical is the search for, and the promotion of, work by persons with the gift to lead our species to a higher stage of mental maturity without destroying the core and content of our humanity. We have to learn to navigate between destructive cynicism and the determination of our decisions by belief in the impossible and illogical. We have to learn to become responsible realists without forgetting that reverence for humankind's inner wealth is needed for our survival as much as air and water.

To that end, Erdmann drew on her extensive reading in future studies, biology, and current affairs, and also encouraged contributions from her readers. Her subscription list, while not large, included many well-known figures, among them the astronomer and science popularizer Eric Chaisson; Robert Muller, longtime assistant secretary general of the United Nations and the UN's unofficial "philosopher in residence"; and, of course, Roger Sperry. Each issue of the quarterly included reviews of relevant books and journal articles, quotations from important thinkers past and present, and Erdmann's own reflections on topics of interest. She continued to publish the journal, without interruption, for more than 15 years. During that time she also wrote another book with me—*A Mind for Tomorrow: Facts, Values, and the Future* (Praeger, 2000), a follow-up to *Beyond a World Divided* which attempted to put Sperry's views in a wider context—and maintained a lively exchange of letters with correspondents the world over. She managed all this despite the loss of her husband, Karl, and deepening health problems as she progressed into her eighties. In one of her last emails to me, she wrote, "Things are fine. Aside from some minor problems—such as increasing breathing difficulties, decline of my eyesight, worsening osteoporosis, constant exhaustion, etc.—my health is absolutely perfect!"

Early in 2006 she wrote to me with news that she was no longer able to live independently. The initial plan was for her to move to British Columbia in order to be nearer to most of her family; a sudden worsening of her health, however, put those plans on hold. In the spring of 2006, she was admitted to hospital in Shelburne, Nova Scotia, where she remained lucid and engaged right to the end. When her children took turns at her bedside reading the most recent issue of *Humankind Advancing* to her (I had taken over editorial duties on the journal by then), she followed closely and commented on the fine points of various articles. But dusk was at hand. Erika Erdmann died, aged 87, on 23 July 2006.

CHAPTER TWO

The Convergence of Science, Religion, and Values

This concise summary of Erdmann's worldview seems an appropriate way to begin. It was submitted to the second Parliament of the World's Religions, held in Chicago in 1993, at the invitation of Dr. Robert Muller.

Humanity's attempts to progress toward a more humane future are blocked by two mutually exclusive worldviews. One segment of our population pursues facts at the expense of values, while another sector is preoccupied with values at the expense of facts. These two worlds, the world of science and the world of religion, are separated by a deep and lethal chasm.

I encountered the depth of this chasm first from the side of science, through Nobel laureate Jacques Monod's "From Biology to Ethics" (1969). This paper recommends the striving for power—not power to achieve a worthwhile goal, but power in itself—as an ethical goal for humans, because it is the dominant principle of non-human reality, which gave rise to the human intellect.

The foreseeable consequences of such a power-dominated ethic have been dramatically described by Aron Kuppermann, professor of chemical physics at the California Institute of Technology, who shocked a lecture audience with the words: "Intelligence is the most dangerous product of evolution!" He explained that intelligence is the result of the fiercest and most ruthless competition in nature, that it is as destructive as the process that brought it about, and that our inability to find intelligent life elsewhere in space is no proof that it has not evolved. Because the universe is 14 billion years old while our earth is only 4½ billion years old, intelligent civilizations might have evolved many times over. But they could not survive. Each time, as soon as a level of mental capability was reached that matched or surpassed our own, their inventions destroyed them.

Were the Caltech physicist's view that of a single scientist, the matter might be dismissed. But it is not. E. J. Chaisson, senior scientist and division head at the Space Telescope Science Institute in Baltimore, Maryland, informs us that quite a number of scientists (though not he) believe that a "cosmic principle of self-destruction" might eliminate all technologically advanced intelligence on any planet, soon after global problems are encountered. The rate of change becomes too rapid for coping; the "drive for complexity" in nature runs out of control.

My experiences of the chasm's depth from its other side—that of religion—were equally disturbing. I will not describe them here. But I believe that if the great founders of the world's religions were with us now, they would implore us to benefit from new facts, new knowledge, and new insights, as well as immemorial wisdom and teachings. They would ask us to break down the walls in which we imprisoned their words and to free the spirit with which they were spoken—the spirit of true concern for the fate of humanity.

With relief I learned that this was indeed being attempted, when I discovered the work of the Institute on Religion in an Age of Science (IRAS), an organization which brings together great thinkers from both science and religion.

Reading the article "Bridging Science and Values: A Unifying View of Mind and Brain" by Roger W. Sperry, published in IRAS's journal *Zygon* in 1979, was a revelation to me. Here a neuroscientist of world renown, a Nobel laureate, merged poetic expression, scientific expertise, original thinking, and a grand vision into a majestic whole. Here I found for the first time his much-quoted words: "Human value priorities . . . stand out as the most strategically powerful causal control now shaping world events. More than any other causal system with which science now concerns itself, it is variables in human value systems that will determine the future."

As a neuroscientist, Sperry provoked his contemporaries through his conviction that "mind moves matter in the brain," not as an outside agent, but as an emergent with new and superior powers. Before he revolted against the neglect of consciousness in science, subjective experience had been generally considered by scientists as an ineffective byproduct of physicochemical activity in neurons (a view which resulted in catastrophic consequences for a meaningful life). –Sperry elevated its importance to that of a leading agent. Only ten years after he had written his pathbreaking papers on the subject in the late sixties, the entire field of behavioral science was turned around. Consciousness, previously considered a subject unsuitable for scientific attention, because a predominant target of research.

The concepts of "emergence" and "downward causation" were crucial for Sperry. He perceived and advanced a new way of thinking where previously an unbridgeable gap existed between physicochemical activity in the brain, which could be objectively observed and described, and our subjective experience of spirituality, values, and meaning, which could not be objectively described and which science had therefore brushed aside.

In Sperry's view, new powers appear during the process of emergence that exert causal effects on properties that had previously evolved (downward causation). Both emergence and downward causation are normal processes of nature. Consider, for example, the situation of living cells carried through the air on the wing of an eagle. The cells alone would not be able to fly; their organization into the wing of a bird makes that feat possible. The properties of the new whole, the bird and its wing, determine the fate of the cells that created it.

According to Sperry's philosophy, every new emergent in the universe affects and influences all previous products of evolution, including those which brought it about. Why should intelligence be an exception? –Perhaps the problem is that most intelligent persons try to solve all difficulties analytically, although some of them can only be solved by intuition.

The Nobel Prize for the discovery that the two halves of the brain work differently—the left hemisphere using the analytical method, and the right one an intuitive all-at-once grasp—had been awarded to Sperry because, according to the Nobel Prize committee, "his work has provided us with an insight into the inner world of the brain which hitherto has almost been hidden from us."

Sperry himself continued to emphasize the cooperation of *both* sides of the brain for healthy and productive thinking, and deplored the fact that the importance of the right hemisphere was being neglected in our educational system.

It is this discovery by science of the right hemisphere's intuitive insights and their value that makes Sperry's work so relevant for our future. It is this discovery, together with Sperry's encompassing vision, that in his 1981 paper "Changing Priorities" moved him to say:

> In the eyes of science, to put it simply, man's creator becomes the vast interwoven fabric of all evolving nature, a tremendously complex concept that includes all the immutable and emergent forces of cosmic causation that control everything from high-energy subnuclear particles to galaxies, not forgetting the causal properties that govern brain function and behavior at individual and social levels. For all these, science has gradually become our accepted authority, offering a cosmic scheme that renders most others simplistic in comparison and which grows and evolves as science advances.

The promise and power of this vision lies in its openness to new knowledge and insights. No imprisonment is more tragic than that of our minds so as to keep out advancing knowledge needed to think and act more responsibly.

Both Sperry's right-hemisphere research and his mind-brain theory led to an amazing increase of mutual understanding between formerly opposed camps. A connection of the right hemisphere with religious experience seemed natural. Monod himself, after studying Sperry's research, maintained that "it is tempting to speculate upon the possibility that the right hemisphere is responsible for an important part, perhaps the most 'profound' part, of subjective stimulation."

In short, it had been found that there was a place in evolution for our depth of thought and feeling that defied all analytical approaches, and that conferred upon us the very essence of being human.

This essence cannot be analytically explained; yet it is easily perceivable and most powerful in human affairs. No proof of its existence is necessary. Even speech is not needed. One can find it across language barriers, across enemy lines. In his book *To Be Human Against All Odds* (1991) the medical doctor, artist, and humanist Frederick Franck said, "Whenever I have met true humanness, and it happened often, I have been moved, often to the point of tears. Each time it has been a revelation to see it in a mere gesture or a glance, to hear it in a word spoken at the right moment."

It is this quality of true humanness and humaneness that is vital for our survival. It is the very quality that negates the cosmic principle of self-destruction.

For this quality reveals previously invisible truths, not only beyond science, but even within science. Progress in evolution appears in a new light. As the great panorama of the ascendance of life is displayed in our minds, we recognize that the most significant advances have occurred not through competition, but through cooperation. Elementary particles, atoms, molecules, living cells, multicellular organisms, societies—all these tell stories of magnificent forward thrusts in evolution made possible by the discovery of compatible constellations among different forces. Our own brains, our own experiences of being free and proud and powerful, are themselves the result of precise and minutely organized interactions of billions of cells, of trillions of atoms and molecules. Cooperation, as much as competition, has brought us to where we are; but emphasis on cooperation is needed to bring us further.

But even if it were not supported by our understanding of evolution, even if it occurred only now for the very first time, the insight that we need to search for compatible constellations among different forces can change our destiny. That is because each time a new thought, a new vision appears on earth, it has the potential to affect the entire world. Philosophers and religious leaders knew this all along. Sperry, through his theory of downward causation, has provided scientific evidence that this phenomenon acts at all levels of reality, and that it can no longer be ignored, even in science. His grand, encompassing vision confers a high value on wisdom, insight, realism, and the courage to break the chains of confined thinking, to break the chains that restrain our initiative to preserve the greatest treasures we have: our beautiful earth, and our threatened quality of being human.

Previous efforts to reconcile science and religion typically demanded that religion adjust to science. For Sperry, the adjustment works both ways. Science has to relinquish its one-sided effort to explain all reality in terms of its smallest possible subdivisions. These divisions simply don't have the characteristics which come into being only through their combinations. Nor will a mere adding-up of particles supply them. New attributes, powers, and potencies appear only through very particular organizations among the particles of a new entity.

It was Sperry's courage and genius to pursue this line of thinking beyond the borders of what had previously been considered scientifically verifiable—into consciousness, subjective experience, and values. He introduced us to a new realm of understanding in which science and religion are both natural components of reality, a reality with a promise and power that did not exist before.

In 1992 a document entitled "World Scientists' Warning to Humanity," signed by 1700 scientists in 70 countries, including 104 Nobel laureates, warned the world of irreversible changes if present trends continue. It concluded:

> A new ethic is required—a new attitude towards discharging our responsibility for caring for ourselves and for the earth. We must recognize the earth's limited capacity to provide for us. We must recognize its fragility. We must no longer allow it to be ravaged. This ethic must motivate a great movement, convincing reluctant leaders and reluctant governments and reluctant peoples themselves to effect the needed changes.

Concern of scientists with ethics has increased from a few isolated persons to a large and growing number. As the vacuum of ethical responsibility in science disappears and religion opens itself toward factual knowledge, a powerful alternative to hitherto stubbornly defended and contrasting world views comes into being. It is a signal of hope that the following words were spoken not by a religious leader but by a leader in science, Roger Sperry:

> *It becomes a logical necessity that humanity be able to perceive itself in terms of a meaningful relation to something more important than itself.*

CHAPTER THREE

Two Key Concepts

Science must find room for the key qualities that make us human—and that make life worth living. This idea was central to Erika Erdmann's worldview. Underpinning it were the concepts of emergence and downward causation, already touched upon in the preceding essay. Erdmann had discussed these ideas at length in her first book, Realism and Human Values. *She then discovered that Roger Sperry had already made use of such concepts in developing a new theory of consciousness, which he had unveiled in the mid-1960s. Erdmann quickly became a vocal and enthusiastic advocate of Sperry's views. In the passage below, these two key concepts are defined and elaborated upon.*

from BEYOND A WORLD DIVIDED (1991)

The concepts of *emergence* and of *downward causation* . . . describe something generally overlooked by reductionistic scientists: the appearance of new laws and properties at every level of organization in nature and the interaction of these laws and properties with all those that had previously evolved.

Instead of a succession of linear cause-effect relationships from particles to brain activity to behavior (with no place for consciousness, values, or meaning) the new worldview takes into account that a complex system of mutual interrelationships exists, in which each new creation becomes a new determining factor. It leads us into a world far more realistic than that of either materialism or dualism.

While the concept of emergence dispenses with any need for external, supernatural powers to account for the phenomenon of creation, it simultaneously demands more respect for the reality and autonomous vigor of new entities than traditional science has allowed. In other words: emergents are not inert; they *act.* They are involved in a constant reshifting of events in our universe. The world of *emergent causation* is the dynamic, living, real world. This is the world in which the emergence of life changed the atmosphere, increased the ratio of oxygen to nitrogen, and led to the . . . rise of oxygen breathers. This is the world in which the emergence of consciousness changed the relationship of man with nature and man with man. This is the world in which the freedom of choice we experience becomes an active factor in evolution.

THE CONCEPT OF EMERGENCE

The *Random House Dictionary* defines *emergence* as "the appearance of new properties in the course of development or evolution that could not have been foreseen at an earlier stage." One example of the process is the appearance of liquidity in water through the combination of hydrogen and oxygen. Water is wet—and "wetness" is an emergent property.

Some critics object that wetness does not exist unless created through the interaction of water molecules with our sense of touch. Nor do taste, sound, light, or colors exist unless taste receptors, ears, or eyes are involved. Therefore, they argue, the entire concept of emergence is questionable. That objection, however, is invalid. Water, undeniably, is able to cause a feeling of wetness when in contact with organs of touch—a property hydrogen or oxygen in isolation do not possess. Taste, sound, light, and colors emerge through the interaction of natural elements with other sense organs. That sense organs are needed to bring them about is no argument against the emergence of these sensations as such.

Whether or not our sense organs are affected by newly emergent properties and characteristics does not change the fact that these properties and characteristics affect one another. With each chance creation of new phenomena through first-time constellations of atoms and molecules, with each new combination of interactions among their forces, new determining factors come into play. For instance, the characteristic of "liquidity" is an emergent property of water that is not dependent on the senses (as opposed to "wetness"). Because of this property of liquidity, water is able to dissolve sodium chloride and form an electrolytic conductor. Neither hydrogen nor oxygen alone is able to do this, yet this has nothing to do with the effect of either on the sense organs.

The concept of emergence itself is not new. The *Encyclopedia Britannica* (fifteenth edition) attributes the first notion of this natural principle to John Stuart Mill, who favored it over *associationism*, the then-dominant view of reality. Under this view, nearly everything we are familiar with is a combination of simpler entities. These components each include a vital aspect, or part, of the new whole. Mill, on the other hand, held that in forming the new whole, the individual parts may well be stripped of their identities, while at the same time the character of the whole object emerges. Wilhelm Wundt termed Mill's notion *creative synthesis*; later yet, it was labeled *emergence*. . . .

Around 1900, the concept was used by the French philosopher Henri Bergson, among others, and ascribed to as yet unknown powers working in the universe, such as the *élan vitale*, a force thought to be connected with living things and distinct from the well-known natural forces studied by physics. Once tainted with mysticism, the entire idea of emergence was rejected by the scientific community, together with everything supernatural or even abstract. Worldviews such as materialism, positivism, and behaviorism, with their extreme concentration on tangible things and their disregard and ridicule of ideals, of values—even of consciousness itself—became dominant. So influential was the unreserved admiration of traditional science's soaring successes in the inorganic and lower organic world, that these views were able to hold the behavioral sciences in their thrall for fifty years, even though they were increasingly perceived as unsatisfactory and the concept of emergence had long since been liberated from its mystical and dualistic connotations.

Sperry's conception of emergence and emergent evolution is fully compatible with modern science. At the same time, he feels that an event or phenomenon can mean something only if the overall guidance of its parts is understood and perceived as emanating from a higher level. If we speak and think about our actions as determined by the physicochemical interplay of atoms and molecules within our brains and bodies, reality remains senseless and nothing will be achieved. Nothing is even worth achieving. But if we speak and think about them in terms of values and ideals, these same events acquire an enormous power and potency—although the laws of nature remain in effect.

THOUGHTS AND IDEAS

Scientists find it difficult to accept the postulate that thoughts and ideas created by the mind—once it has emerged from brain activity—interact with one another at their own level. Is Sperry really thinking of the mind in a dualistic sense after all: disembodied, divorced from the physical brain, and inhabitant of a world apart?

Quite the contrary. Sperry has repeatedly emphasized that the mind is inevitably tied to, and a part of, the living brain. Thus, while thoughts and ideas in the mind interact at their own level, physical and chemical changes in the brain occur simultaneously. The crucial difference between Sperry and materialistic neuroscientists is that he sees mental interaction as a newly emerged phenomenon of primary importance, with chemical changes being secondary; while materialists argue that events occur the other way around, with physical and chemical changes of first importance and mental action a superfluous byproduct.

In Sperry's view, decisions produced through conscious effort guide the organization of brain activity in a way that would be impossible without such effort. All cultural achievements are results of conscious thought and could not have occurred without it.

That does not make Sperry's position a dualistic one. He retains a one-world view in which each newly emergent phenomenon is causally active—from atoms formed from nuclear particles to the most profound ideals created by the functioning of the brain at a level beyond which our physical investigations can reach: the level of the mind.

THE CONCEPT OF DOWNWARD CAUSATION

Sperry himself considers the concept of *downward causation* his own most significant contribution to the understanding of the mind-brain relationship and to the philosophy of ethics.

Downward causation describes how the properties of the whole determine the fate of its parts—parts whose organization created the whole to begin with. The relationship is always a two-way street: mutual, reciprocal, and simultaneous. That is, downward causation does not *supplant* the laws and properties associated with single parts; instead, it provides a new and more dominant *organizing principle.* As Sperry sees it, *mental properties*—thoughts, values, and so forth—do not intervene in the functioning of individual brain cells. Rather, they *supervene.* To supervene means to give overall direction to physical processes without disturbing them, in much the same way that a computer program directs the machine's output or a television program controls the patterns of light and dark formed on the screen (examples used by Sperry in several of his papers).

Using more current philosophical terms, Sperry has spoken of *micro-properties* (properties of the parts) being overridden by *macro-properties* (properties of the whole).

> What matters is that the movement and fate of the parts . . . once the whole is formed, are thereafter governed by entirely new macro-properties and laws that previously *did not exist*, because they are properties of a new configuration.

For instance, consider the situation of living cells carried through the air in the wing of an eagle. The cells alone would not be able to fly; their organization into the wing of a bird makes that feat possible. The properties of the new whole, the bird and its wing, determine the fate of the cells that created it. Or consider a forest. The size and shape of each tree is determined by the proximity of other trees around it. The accumulation of humus in the ground depends upon trees providing enough protection from the wind to keep leaves from blowing away. The moisture content, amount of shade or sunshine, and the flora and fauna within a forest are all determined by properties of the forest as a whole, while at the same time each of these particulars, as it affects the others, becomes a co-creator of this one entity: the forest. It is this wonderful, near-mythical interweaving of causes and effects, in which being, becoming, and creating are one, that underlies the phenomena of emergence and downward causation.

Sperry's favorite example is that of a wheel rolling downhill and carrying its atoms and molecules along, "whether they like it or not." Since that example can be explained through the exact knowledge of single-part properties—those of the wheel, the hill, the earth's gravity, and so on—it has often been rejected as too simplistic and as making the concept of downward causation superfluous. Downward causation acquires its full significance only where the complexity of the situation and the accumulation of unknowns make all other explanations crude distortions of reality.

CHAPTER FOUR

Resolving the Antagonism Between Emotion and Reason

Even before moving to California to work with Sperry, Erdmann had thought long and hard about the relationship between emotion and reason. To be fully human, she believed, is both to feel and to think; only the combination of the two allows us to completely realize our potentialities. In Realism and Human Values, *she discussed in detail the antagonism between these two ways of looking at and interacting with the world. The roots of the conflict, she decided, are found deep in our prehuman past; and in understanding our evolutionary heritage, she hoped, we might find ways to overcome the age-old antagonism between emotion and reason. In the following excerpt from* Realism and Human Values, *the development of foresight and long-range planning are traced. Without the gift of reason, Erdmann concludes, we lack the ability to act fully and effectively in response to the tug of our emotions. Without our emotions to drive us, we lack the initiative to act at all.*

from REALISM AND HUMAN VALUES (1978)

No purposive activity can occur where choice of action is absent, and no choice of action can occur without a source of direction that is sensitive to the results of the activity and that is able to memorize those results. The nervous systems of higher animals and of humans are the only organs capable of such feats. In man alone, foresight is extended into the capacity for long-range planning.

In lower animals, love involves only hormones and sense stimulants; in higher animals it involves learning as well; in man it involves, in addition to all other prerequisites, reason and foresight. They must be present to create a world that permits the expression of human love. They must be present to extend reciprocal altruism beyond the limited circle of human contacts for which we are prepared by those ancestral impulses that are elicited by our emotions.

The devastating results of love without reasoning are exemplified by the behavior of creatures without sufficient brain capacity. The blackcap, a small migratory bird, is able to find its way over hundreds of miles into distant parts of the earth, navigating by the stars. It is, however, unable to solve the simplest problems for which its behavioral repertoire is not prepared. When a cuckoo intruder pushes the blackcap's own young out of the nest, or just onto the rim from where it could easily be brought back to warmth and security by a flick of the beak, the bird mother will do nothing but warm and feed the culprit, snuggling comfortably beside her own dying young. Such cruelty in a creature that normally knows nothing but tenderness for its offspring and that hardly dares to eat or rest during the care for a nestful of fledglings, can only be explained by the observation that the stimulus of an open beak alone determines the direction of her motherly love—nothing else.

Reasoning does not occur in birds, although they have several layers of cells corresponding to the neocortex, the newest layer of the "bark" of the brain, which itself grew over the previous bark, the paleocortex, a structure that superseded the even older archicortex. Nor does reasoning occur in rats, where the cortex contains the first, hardly noticeable association regions, that is, regions neither primarily occupied with sensory input or motor output. Even the first creases and convolutions that increase cortical area in higher mammals are not yet correlated with reasoning, except for the first rudimentary beginnings in apes.

In man, where the neocortex alone accounts for two-thirds of the weight of the brain, the capacity to reason is fully developed. Astonishingly, however, IQ scores are not affected even by quite serious damage to the cortical association areas. Except in early childhood, when the infant learns how to learn and how to relate to the world, and when brain damage has very serious consequences, man seems to be able to get along rather well without an intact cortex. For instance, the only defects after injury of the frontal association areas are impairments in social sensitivity and loss of long-range planning ability. The frontal lobes seem to be involved in the finer regulation of emotion in the same way as the cortical motor regions are involved in the finer regulation of muscle activity. Long-range planning ability is found in the lateral parts of the front lobes, in the sulcus principalis, a convolution that was one of the last to evolve. With it, purposive action was finally able to encompass lifelong projects.

Normal thought is intimately interwoven with emotional and motivational components. Although both halves of the brain are connected with each other, there are relatively few short lateral interconnections within each half of the neocortex. Most connections lead downward into the older parts of the brain and upward again from these parts. It seems, therefore, probable that pure reasoning involves inhibition of emotional interference. Such an assumption is supported by observation of human behavior. When strong emotions like fear or love are being experienced, reasoning becomes impossible. It is also impossible for young children and for adults under the influence of drugs, alcohol, or hypnosis. The process of reasoning seems to demand intense concentration. Without motivation from the older parts of the brain, however, no reasoning can be initiated. No purposive action is possible without involvement of the entire nervous system.

THE EMERGENCE OF MIND

When life first began, the slightest change in the environment led to the death of the organism. The organism's internal workings could not adjust to take advantage of different external conditions. As life evolved and advanced, two characteristics were favored: the ability to change internal reactions to suit external changes, and the ability to change the external environment. Primitive organisms use *taxis* (chemical guidance of movement) to transport their bodies into regions of optimal metabolic function. Advanced organisms use memory, pain, and pleasure to direct their activity.

While the response of a very simple creature without a nervous system depends entirely upon the stimulus and is elicited automatically as from a machine, an ever increasing response repertoire becomes available with the growth of the brain and development of the faculty of memory. The neural pathway from stimulus to response is intercepted and its activity changed by an ever increasing reservoir of neurons whose rate of firing has been permanently altered by previous experience. It becomes possible to anticipate change and prepare for it. As the repertoire of responses increases and choice becomes more difficult, purposive action coordinates all activity to obtain a preconceived goal. Ethics, emerging much later, is concerned with the choice of that goal.

There is no point where the mind enters the body, just as there is no point at which life enters into non-living chemicals. The mind is an emergent property of non-living matter.

The common objection to such a view is based on the erroneous conclusion it degrades mind to nothing more than matter and life to mere chemistry. Such a conclusion disregards the emergence of new properties that are entirely different from their constituents. When hydrogen and oxygen atoms combine to form water, changes occur which bring into existence something new that has thoroughly different characteristics from those of the atoms that formed it. But nothing was added from outside: water is made up only of its constituent hydrogen and oxygen atoms. Similar, only of infinitely more complexity and impact, are the changes that that led from non-living to living matter and from living matter to conscious experience.

There is nothing extra-worldly about the change of properties in chemical combinations, nothing that is not inherent in all matter. No mysteries are involved, except for the one great mystery: the existence of energy; the existence of the tendency to act. The properties of atoms and molecules in the gaseous state result from the speed of their movement, which leaves no time for the weaker cohesive forces to become effective—as they are in a liquid or solid. The latter differs from the former again only by the degree of independence of single atoms. In a liquid, cohesive bonds are not strong enough to resist attempts of exterior gravity to separate its parts; in a solid, they are. Other properties such as color or texture are based on the reflection or absorption of portions of the light spectrum or on the particular arrangements of atoms in a solid.

Matter itself is an emergent property of energy. Subatomic particles do not have to be matter to create matter, nor do atoms have to be alive to create life. Life is an emergent property of a certain configuration and interplay of a great many atoms, just as matter is an emergent property of the interplay of forces of energy. Similarly, thoughts and emotions are emergent properties of energy interplay in the brain, and the experience of values and meaning in life is the result of thought and emotion. It cannot be concluded that life does not exist because atoms are not living. Neither can it be concluded that values or meaning in life do not exist because they cannot be found by dissecting the brain. But it is just as wrong to conclude that life could exist without atoms, or that values could exist without the human brain.

The acceptance of the scientific view of the emergence of man's mind depends upon the understanding that newly emerged properties are something completely different from the entities that built them.

ALTRUISM IN ANIMALS

No correlation exists in the animal world between phylogenetic advance of a species and altruistic behavior. It occurs wherever the interplay between organism and environment demands its presence for the animal's survival. It is absent wherever survival is possible without it.

One-celled creatures may devour each other; they may combine temporarily or permanently into multicellular organisms. Insects can be extremely cruel to each other; they can show a high degree of cooperation. A female spider or praying mantis will feed on its own partner after mating; wasps, bees, ants, and termites work ceaselessly for each other and their young.

Although all behavior at this stage of evolution is purely mechanical and mostly determined by pheromones, chemical particles that act on the organs of smell or taste, it is no coincidence that many species forming large societies based on altruism evolved independently in the hymenoptera. All sterile workers in this order are more closely related to each other than brothers and sisters. An ant-worker, for instance, shares three-quarters of its genes with its fellow workers, while in most organisms, including insects, only half the genes are shared by siblings. In such insects, advanced sociality has arisen only once (with the termites). Similarity of genetic makeup seems to be conducive to the emergence of systems that recognize and act upon the needs of another organism of the same species.

In higher animals, like birds or mammals, the brain is more highly developed than in insects, and the dependence of behavior upon immediate stimuli is modified by experience and memory. Such animals can learn to alter their instinctual tendencies, although usually with much difficulty. As in lower species, their natural behavior encompasses both cruelty and altruism.

The lioness, for instance, has to do most of the killing of the prey, only to be chased away by her stronger mate who then gorges himself and does not permit her near the kill until his hunger has been satisfied. She, in turn, chases her cubs away and does not permit them to eat until she has had her fill. Whenever a scarcity of food develops, the young are the first to die of starvation. The African hunting dog, on the other hand, roaming through the same savanna and hunting similar prey, has developed care for the weaker members of its group to the utmost. The adults will leave their prey as soon as the young appear on the scene of the kill, and wait till the young have had enough. They will regurgitate their own food for the use of the smallest pups living near the burrows, for nursing females, and even for hungry hunting mates. Single dogs without the urge to hunt could survive well in such a group; if their demands exceeded the feeding capacity of the hunters, however, the whole community might succumb to malnourishment. In spite of this danger, group solidarity has priority in the hunting dog because, in contrast to the lion, a single dog would not be able to overcome the big ungulates that are the prey and sustenance of his species.

It is necessity, not the size of the brain, that determines the degree of altruism present in a species. The animal's activity, of course, does not depend on its understanding that necessity. The urge to act is determined by its nervous system, and the structure of that nervous system is determined by the way the animal's genes prepared it to interact with its environment. Joy probably accompanies instinctual behavior in all warm-blooded animals. Such an assumption is supported by animal observation, by extrapolation from the human feelings of joy and relief that are correlated with the release of impulse action from suppression, and by the animal's incessant self-stimulation of "pleasure centers" of the brain. The main location of these pleasure centers coincides with that of a bundle of neural pathways involved in species-specific behavior patterns governing such activities as eating, drinking, gnawing, copulation, and hunting. Much of animal behavior is indeed hard to explain unless an element of satisfaction in the pure acting-out of instinctual behavior is assumed. Why otherwise would a cat play with a dying mouse?

An animal in its natural habitat is attuned to its environment. It can act according to its impulses and at the same time do what is best for its survival; all detrimental instincts have been eliminated by the death of their bearers. Only where learning has advanced to such overwhelming importance as it has in the human species, only where detrimental impulses can be suppressed while their bearers continue to live and reproduce—only there is a separation between desired action and right action possible.

THE NON-HUMAN PRIMATES

Groups of non-human primates have been studied widely and with special interest. Is it possible to find the origin of human behavior hidden in their interactions? The answer is positive but disappointing. Some aspects of their habits are surprisingly similar to human behavior, but to human behavior at its worst. Humans are, of course, primates ourselves; but for convenience the term "primate" will be used here to refer to non-human members of the order.

As in many species, dominance hierarchies are firmly established. Generally, the strongest animal claims the best place, the best food, the first access to a favorite female. The leader will hit, bite, and terrorize any weaker member of his group who is not subservient. The next strongest primate will show gestures of respect to his superior, but dominate the rest of the group. The third in line fears the two superiors and terrorizes everyone else. The pattern continues until the last, a nervous and half-starved weakling, is attacked at the least provocation by every other member of the group. The females have to suffer from the stronger males, but they protect their infants. Only after young apes are old enough to leave their mothers are they persecuted and pushed toward the fringes of the group. A weaker member of the group may be attacked by a stronger one even without provocation. It has been observed, for instance, that in two primate groups confronting each other, either of the two leaders may vent his aggressive mood on an inferior of his own group instead of on the stronger enemy whom he does not dare attack. Ordinarily, however, peace prevails once each animal's place in the dominance hierarchy is established. Weaker animals learn the skill of keeping out of the way of the stronger ones or showing them gestures of subservience at all possible opportunities. Permanent respect may be shown, though, to the weak offspring of strong, aggressive, and protective females.

Although the meaning of each particular gesture is very similar throughout a primate species, the individuality of the single animal, and the influence of its individuality on the group, is most remarkable; it is this, more than anything else, that foreshadows the uniqueness of human behavior. Patterns of conduct are far less predetermined than in lower species. In one group, a superior may suffer young monkeys beside him and even permit them to eat while he eats; in another group of the same species, the leader inhibits all such attempts. These different behavioral patterns are thought to be perpetuated for generations. An air of comfort and mutual friendship prevails in the first group, an air of tension and fear in the second, but chances for survival are the same in both.

Of great interest is the question of whether divergent individual behavior in the same species is the consequence of experience or of differences in the construction of the nervous system. Investigations support the opinion that both of these are influential determinants of behavior. Monkeys, reared without mothers, siblings, or other animal contact, will resist mating, and if females are forced to do so and produce offspring, they will lack all motherly instincts, push their young away, and treat them like parasites. Normal mating and maternal behavior occur in primates only if the joy of being touched has been experienced in early youth. Nevertheless, experience is to no avail if the brain lacks the structures necessary for its processing.

If the amygdala, the part of the brain that interprets the meaning of visual input, is damaged in a young monkey, the animal is unable to learn appropriate behavior toward other members of the dominance hierarchy. It will approach superiors confidently, is unable to interpret threatening or display-soliciting gestures, and cannot tell friend from foe. As a result, it will in its natural habitat be bitten and mutilated by members of its own group as well as enemy groups, which it lacks the sense to avoid, until it succumbs to its wounds.

The idea of justice—the idea that, independent of a degree of relationship or knowledge, no one should be the target of contempt and hatred, simply because he is weak—is unknown to any primate but man. The way from stimulus-bound acts of compassion to imagining oneself in another creature's place must wait for the emergence of thought and fantasy.

MAN: THE EMERGENCE OF FANTASY

No direct observation of the evolution of man's subjective experience is possible. Some inferences, however, can be drawn from man's earliest ritual burials, sculptures, and cave paintings; from the observation of present-day hunter and gatherer groups; and from cults and customs as well as tales of magic and mystical experience that have been transmitted from generation to generation since prehistoric time. Another source of inference is the expression of subjective experience as related by young children, and also our own fantasies. Sometimes we feel the urgent need to relate something of importance to our fellows, yet no words seem to have been invented for that which we wish to express. It is at such moments that we feel closest to the mental experience of our earliest ancestors.

Of relevance in this respect is the report of a French explorer about his life with a pack of huskies in the Arctic. These dogs establish dominance hierarchies through vicious fighting, but the strongest animal, the victor and subsequent leader of the pack, was not always the most intelligent. The explorer reports that the pack, when hitched to a sled and commanded to go in a certain direction, was always confused by the leader, who was never able to learn the proper meaning of the commands and most of the time headed off in the wrong direction. Then a mixed-up scramble with fighting and biting would take place, into which every dog joined except for one, a slender animal of medium strength and very high intelligence. This dog always lined itself up in the right direction at the moment the command was given and stood patiently waiting until the dominant husky noticed it. The leader then lined himself up beside his more intelligent subservient and thus gave the signal for the entire pack to take off in the desired direction. The same scramble and same solution occurred several times daily for many years.

In a similar way, early men of more-than-average intelligence must have led the way through confusion and irrational behavior, just by acting as living examples to their fellows. Long before the first thought-out guidelines for action occurred to men, long before the first words were spoken, humans must already have been subject to rules of behavior, to habits, transmitted by example. These habits and rules must have been good ones, or neither man nor thought would have come into being. The survival of a species with an unusually long period of infant dependency must have required mutual love and care together with the joy of the chase and of killing.

Prolonged child care was the precondition for an increase in brain size and memory, which in turn released an abundance of stored pictures in dreams and daydreams. It is very probable that early man did not always clearly differentiate between dream and reality, and that his world was filled with spirits. As in the world of a young child, there were fear-induced evil spirits and friendly, helpful ones. Sometimes man could see them fighting with each other. Internal vision was sharpened by his cruel struggle with nature; haunted by hunger and pain-filled, sleepless nights, he saw apparitions unknown to us. His instincts regressing, his knowledge still limited, primitive man clung to his visions to govern his daily life. Gifts and sacrifices were thought helpful to gain the favor of mysterious powers. Rituals, deeply stirring events, sometimes including sadistic mutilations and human sacrifices, were transmitted from generation to generation together with sacred stories and revered customs. Irrelevant or even detrimental habits and taboos mingled with useful teachings. But only the dominance of the latter led to the survival of the group.

For many thousands of years, habits that allowed a steady increase in brain size must have preceded the full bloom of fantasy and the emergence of speech and thought. When speech and thought developed step-by-step in alternation, the internal and external worlds were not at first clearly separated. Man was sometimes startled, even frightened by his own thoughts, which he experienced as voices from the wind, the trees, the animals around him. Nature and the ferocious beasts that filled man's imagination were his guiding spirits. With perfection of speech and thought, however, interactions with other human beings increasingly lingered in man's mind, causing his spirits to lose their animal or half-animal bodies and turn into gods that resembled men.

Gods were never merely manlike, however; they always embodied mystical powers, they always combined man's highest aspirations, his dreams, his hopes, with his view of reality. Man heard his God speak to him and did not know it was the conclusions and realizations occurring in his own subconscious mind that appeared to him suddenly in the form of exciting and awe-inspiring intuitions. Man's contemplations about the best way of life led his God to pronounce moral laws.

The best of these laws extended cooperation and mutual care from small groups to larger ones and finally led roaming bands into nationhood. Permanent occupation of fertile land led to the awareness of increased security, to the anticipation and organization of leisure time, to the enjoyment of the creation and accumulation of beautiful things, and to the invention of writing. Writing was used to store records of customs and moral laws.

Wherever moral laws were written down for many thousands of years in succession, it is possible to trace the influence of wise and thoughtful men on the way the character of their nation's God was perceived. The God of the Old Testament, for instance, slowly over time changes from a revenge-hungry tyrant in the oldest parts of the book into a loving father. Compassion, the ability of man to imagine himself in the place of another person, to feel what he feels, to suffer what he suffers, has eliminated sadism from all major religions and replaced it with the command to care for one's neighbor.

While God worked through the thoughts of men, however, eternities separated the human and the divine. Myths and morals mingled in man's mind, forming indivisible entities, deeply revered and far above man's ability to judge. To question the rationality of a myth or the validity of a moral code was in itself a crime.

THE EMERGENCE OF LOGICAL THOUGHT

Although historical evidence of logical thought appears later than written records or moral laws, intertwined in mythical imagery, man must have started to think systematically as soon as conscious decision-making began to replace actions governed by instincts. The construction of useful tools, the employment of words and concepts to plan a group hunt, and many other activities of our early ancestors suggest the ability of their brains to organize past experience, to draw conclusions, to extrapolate, and to guide activity accordingly. In fact, the emergence of systematic thinking seems to have been far more necessary than the emergence of fantasy, which continually interferes with the use of reason and occasionally endangers man's very survival. Yet fantasy is universal in man and an intimate part of being human.

Fantasy and intuitive knowledge appear in man's consciousness as the result of interactions of experience with older parts of the brain, those which govern such essential but unconscious physical activity as breathing, digestion, the heartbeat, and many hormonal secretions. Without the older parts of the brain, no motivation for any activity would exist. Without the neocortex, however, action would be irrational and disastrous.

Those neurons and their organization that led to the subjective experience of consciousness and systematic thought led simultaneously to the survival of all the detrimental variations of the nervous system whose activity could be suppressed, when needed, by reason. Man's world became richer, he became more imaginative and inventive, but he could not live any longer without being able to select among conflicting impulses.

Logical thought leads to conclusions and realizations as an end result of a succession of mental processes carried out entirely in that part of man's mind of whose work he is conscious. Such conclusions and realizations can be proved right or wrong by following each step of the mental procedure. Two persons can compare their thoughts with each other, debates can take place, and it becomes possible to convince a person through the power of logic to change his mind rather than to expect or force him to believe something contrary to his own convictions.

To take full advantage of the capacity for logical reasoning, it is necessary that the language center be intact and sufficiently evolved to permit communication of ideas to other people and to profit from their reactions, and that there be several persons at the same time capable of understanding each other. It is probable that many intelligent men have been tortured and destroyed because of the incomprehension of their fellow creatures, and that many more have preferred silence to the expression of their thoughts, sometimes living out their entire lifetimes unknowingly alongside like-minded individuals, before logic and courage started to evaluate the products of fantasy and began to lift, for the first time, the veil of fear and irrationality from the fate of man.

Such an event must have preceded the flowering of systematic thought in ancient Greece, where within a small group of cities over a few hundred years such an abundance of originality was stimulated that all later philosophical speculation in the Western world rests on concepts developed by the ancient Greeks. Administration and law were inspired by Greek teachers who were in demand throughout the Roman Empire, Christian teachings incorporated Greek moral thought, political rulers were influenced by Greek ideas of statecraft, and many modern scientific theories were foreshadowed by the intuitive hypotheses of Greek natural philosophers. Greek discoveries in mathematics, geometry, and logic survived without change into modern times. Overwhelmed by the power of reason, however, the Greeks neglected to realize the immense importance of the premises upon which logic is based. They were unaware that logic, based on wrong premises, can be just as disastrous as unchecked intuition—or even more so. They did not initiate the centuries of repeated, patient, painstaking comparison of logical extrapolations with observed facts that much later led to the discovery of the extended and interconnected body of reliable knowledge that constitutes modern science. Their eyes were blind to the importance of empirical investigations because these demanded manual labor, thought to be worthy only of slaves and not free men. To clear the path for the great discoveries of the age of science, slavery had to be abolished first. The abolishment of slavery, however, came about because of intuitive ethics—not logic.

THE STRUGGLE BETWEEN FANTASY AND LOGIC

Logic did not supplant intuitive ethics; on the contrary, all attempts to use a strictly objective scientific method to arrive at a code of conduct have failed. Even were computers to be used for this purpose, the outcome would still be hopeless. Astonishing results have been achieved in all fields amenable to the manipulation of quantitative measurements. Man's knowledge has expanded far beyond his most ambitious dreams of only a few decades ago. He has walked on the moon, he has invented the means to abolish on earth hunger and most diseases, but he has also developed the capacity to destroy all life on our planet. What will he do? Logic, alone, is completely unable to answer that question.

What the Greeks did not know, and could not have known, is the decisive role played by emotion in all thought concerned with human problems. They were unaware of the importance of older brain structures and their interactions, of decisions that reach the conscious mind with the impact of revelations, of the motivational power of these decisions, and of the immense importance such revelations had throughout man's development. Emotions were thought to be irrational, worthy only of contempt.

This vacuum created by Greek rationalism's disregard of man's need for emotional satisfaction attracted a new religion from the south. There were promises of eternal joy for the desperate, and threats of terrible punishment after death to deter wickedness. Worry was calmed by trust in God's wisdom and concern. There were myths to fill the imagination and elicit awe. All this contributed to the success of humanity. Its main power, however, came from the new idea that any human being, whether rich or poor, male or female, master or slave, possesses an intrinsic value just by being human, just by being able to love and care. Man's natural goodness, ridiculed in favor of courage by the hunter, in favor of efficiency by the farmer, and in favor of knowledge by the sophist, was not only permitted to assert itself, it was thought to be man's greatest asset.

But now the problem was only reversed, not solved. Again, only part of man's needs were satisfied. No integration took place. Attractive as the appeal of Christianity was to hungry human emotion, it left the mind wanting. Moral codes were intertwined with myth, the questioning of which led to the most severe punishment. It was feared that inquisitive thought would destroy morals together with myths. The quest for knowledge was choked by fanatical righteousness mingled with pure devotion, or, since the Church had been infiltrated by greedy, cruel, and power-hungry individuals as soon as persecution of Christians in the Roman Empire ended, also with malevolence. Side by side with the saints, villains impressed their image on the Middle Ages. The inability to live with contradictions was seen as demonic, and with the devil within him, the searcher for truth was tortured, burned, and killed. Again, a veil of fear and irrationality covered the earth.

Eventually some of the writings of the Greek philosophers were rediscovered. A kind of truncated reasoning became fashionable after the Crusades. Logic was used to explain God's ways, but was turned and twisted as soon as it contradicted the Bible. Man was allowed to think systematically only until he reached an impenetrable barrier. Later, when thinking became more daring, the discovery of laws of nature was carefully justified as contributing to the glory of God. Only when the use of the scientific method, of strictly controlled, repeatable experiments, led to surprising success in the relief of suffering and the elimination of squalor, did the search for reality itself become respectable.

Once theological impediments had been overcome, all superstitions, the results of untested projections from inaccurate observations, were separated from repeatedly and carefully tested phenomena. The foundation was laid for the first glimpse of a surprisingly interrelated body of knowledge available to man. Scientific discoveries were now greeted with optimism, and hope for undreamt-of benefits from science spread over the earth. The overcoming of all pain, fear, and squalor would only be a matter of time: it was taken for granted that men would soon be able to resolve their differences by means of logical discussions rather than wars.

These hopes, however, remained unfulfilled. Wars became more devastating, the beauty of the environment was destroyed, loved ways of life were changed. Greedy, cruel, and power-hungry individuals used science as they had used religion.

Their hopes disappointed, men changed their attitudes again. Unable to recognize the roots of their problems in the irrationality of human desires, they rejected the only faculties that could assist them: man's capacity for reason and logic. Confidence in value judgments, however, had vanished long ago, and without constant stimulation, life appeared empty and senseless. The desperate struggle of a few exceptional persons to solve present-day problems has little support. The overwhelming majority retreats into fantasy before a reality that seems to have become unbearable to contemplate, and many of man's mental powers wither unused.

RESOLVED ANTAGONISM

Both reason and emotion are necessary components of the human thought process; to remain human, both must be cultivated. If we want beauty, we must create and preserve it; if we want love, we must create a world that makes its expression possible. The relation between science and ethics may be compared with the relation between a lone wanderer's ability to breathe and his ability to see, lost in the treacherous peaks and precipices of an icy mountain range. Without breathing, he cannot live; without seeing, he cannot survive. He could close his eyes and wait for paralysis before freezing to death. His eyes had lured him, his eyes had shown him only the beauty and challenge of the cloud-covered peaks, and he may curse his eyes—but he cannot return without using them.

It is not necessary to repudiate logic in order to feel reverence for those values that are at the core of every higher religion. It is not necessary to reject the theory of evolution in order to avoid the inhuman ruthlessness of relentless competition. Conclusions drawn from laws that govern the activity of inorganic substances and of subhuman life do not and cannot govern the activities of man—not because those laws are wrong, not because man did not evolve from other animals—but precisely because evolution did take place and because it did not end after our prehuman ancestors appeared on the earth; precisely because through the emergence of man, evolution was influenced by completely new factors never before present on earth: man's conscious experience of love, his capacity for extended foresight, and his will to determine his own fate.

The antagonism between science and religion is not only fatal, it is unnecessary. Man became human because the interaction of atoms and molecules within his brain gave rise to those emotions and thoughts that led to the rejection of the idea of mutual obliteration of which his intelligence makes him capable. That counterbalance must be maintained. The rejection of reason and logic by concerned humanists would not avoid the dangers of misguided technology; it would merely leave the most powerful tools in the hands of the most ruthless people. To retain our world, we must understand it. No beauty exists, no joy, no purpose, no meaning in life, without a brain to experience them—nor without an environment to which that brain can respond.

Religion is an expression of essential human emotions, using dogma, parables, and myth to convey a meaning for which as yet no words exist. Dogma, legend, and myth can be compared with a framework, or with a chalice, that contains what is holy to mankind. The form of a specific religion is as inessential as the form of a chalice in relation to its content. Not what a man professes to believe is important, but how his belief affects his actions. It is possible to completely disregard the chalice and to concentrate on its content alone—to act thoughtfully and justly without professing any religion—but to shatter the chalice with contempt and misunderstanding leads to the loss of its content for those who need formulated guidance. Religious fanaticism, on the other hand, is indifferent to the content of the chalice; it concentrates on its form alone.

Science, unless consciously or unconsciously guided by human warmth and concern, can be extremely dangerous. Science is power. But it is also the power to prevent the extinction of man, the extinction of love. Science sets limits to fantasy. Thus it can prevent the sacrifice of entire populations for unattainable goals. More than anything else, science is light. It enables man to walk toward the darkness of the future, knowing which chasms to avoid.

To resolve the antagonism between emotion and reason, the need for both must be understood. Only emotion initiates action, only emotion determines its direction, and only emotion provides the power to conquer nearly insurmountable obstacles. But the success of any undertaking is determined by the balance between emotion and reason; reason alone prevents senseless suicide.

CHAPTER FIVE
Love Is Not Enough

Realist that she was, Erdmann understood that while the capacity for love was one of humanity's greatest gifts, love alone is not enough to build a constructive, compassionate world. Without the benefit of foresight and objective knowledge, love is all too often blind—and to borrow a phrase from the Bible, "if the blind lead the blind, both shall fall into the ditch" (Matthew 15: 14).

from REALISM AND HUMAN VALUES (1978)

The attempt to build unrealistic utopias has been paid for with countless lives. Religions have failed. Political systems have failed. The building of new utopias is senseless without a thorough knowledge of human nature and its sources.

A drastic example of the misjudgment of human powers is the burning of witches at the end of the Middle Ages. It was believed that disasters such as hurricanes and shipwrecks were caused by the evil magic of witches. Only when science discovered the real reasons for such disasters were mental powers judged more realistically and the burnings ceased.

Nevertheless, it is still lack of knowledge that leads to terrible injustices. For instance, a widespread belief maintains that the only action necessary to improve man's lot would be the removal of all authority. Man is good by nature, and all crime is simply the result of repression. Even if that assumption were true, friction through incompatible desires cannot be eliminated, even when only a few people live together. But in most places on earth, more than just a few people must live together. Suppression of impulses is unavoidable and essential, and not everyone has the good sense to do this voluntarily. Obviously, however, it is not as easy to leave the earth as it is to leave a small rural community, and the problem has to be dealt with. The objection that at least most men are good and that lack of common sense is an exception—again assuming that this is true—does not help either. Even a minimal amount of unreason must lead to suppression, either of others or by others—and the viciousness that had just been eliminated from the world is created anew. In the absence of all law, however, not much viciousness is needed to create the most widespread and appalling results. Deceit and terror, masterminded by very few persons, have led to dramatic changes in history in the past and still occur. There are some places on earth where a few families live together in harmony, separated from the rest of society, but their lives are regulated by tradition and religion. Moreover, there are many families, also living together in isolated groups, where heartlessness and greed dominate communal interaction. Unfortunately, it is probable that cruelty and craving for power are just as much part of human nature as kindness and compassion, both guiding man's activity since his evolution from lower forms of life. Certainly the former qualities are very much part of non-human nature.

Defenders of a return to a life more in accord with nature emphasize nature's tendency to balance and harmony rather than competition, and point out that the welfare of one species depends on the welfare of all others in its environment, even its natural enemies. But it is precisely nature's way of maintaining that balance which is perceived as cruel by man and which he rejects. Predators roam the savannas and devour the sick, the weak, the single gazelles, leaving a healthy and vigorous herd with communal instincts intact. Spider wasps paralyze spiders and lay their eggs on the defenseless body, which serves, while still alive, as food for the emerging larvae. To make sure that the spider is completely defenseless, even if it should regain its ability to move before it is completely devoured, the wasps go so far as to amputate the spider's legs after it is paralyzed. That is how nature achieves its harmony! Should these methods be examples for us? Could they be examples for any living being that is capable of sensation and emotion? —Never! —Diversity, balance, and harmony are desirable, but man must devise his own methods to reach these aims.

The belief in man's natural goodness is balanced by three other beliefs: man is evil; he has no nature at all; his nature is mainly determined by his genes. The belief that man is evil by nature, that all his impulses and desires must be suppressed, destroyed, rooted out, and replaced by the experience of God's grace and love in order to forge him into a good, kind person, a belief that was widespread during the Middle Ages, the Reformation, and indeed only a hundred years ago, is fortunately now nearly absent.

On the other hand, it is still widely believed that there is no human nature at all, except for the one created by conditioning and learning. Man is infinitely malleable like water, and everyone can be taught everything. All our problems are caused by inefficient teaching methods and undefined goals. Such a belief is contrasted with the view that innate character traits are rigidly fixed. Both sides attack each other violently, all in the absence of knowledge about human nature.

It would, of course, be inhuman to acquire knowledge about man's nature through specially designed experiments, but careful observations and records of all chance designs in human life can provide much information, as long as these observations are reported with objectivity, and generalization from isolated and uncommon experiences is avoided. Chance designs may include the reaction of single persons to individual situations, however, as well as the reaction of entire populations to social change. The introduction of any new political system can be viewed as a grand design to test human nature, and far less bloodshed would occur if such a view prevailed. In reality, however, revolutionary changes are accompanied by such furious emotions that objective records are difficult to obtain after the fact.

Even in peaceful times, the study of human nature encounters strong emotions and prejudices. It is very probable that an immense diversity of talents and aptitudes exists, and that every individual has a propensity to learn certain things while he has difficulties with others. The fear of acknowledging such differences is mainly based on the existence of a single measure of human worth: intelligence. Kindness and human warmth, attributes of the greatest importance, are not considered. However, no human problems can be solved without genuine care for humanity. Intelligence, as measured by tests, may be far removed from real insight. The objective study of human nature and the acknowledgement of differences would be easier if such differences did not imply contempt for some persons but instead formed the basis for creating a society in which every individual fulfilled a worthwhile function. The creation of a good society is impossible without a thorough knowledge of human nature, and such knowledge can only be gained with genuine good intentions.

It becomes increasingly apparent that experiences during earliest infancy decisively direct all later events in a person's life. For instance, an infant that has been deaf until the age of two years and then becomes able to hear will never learn to speak properly. But an infant that has been able to hear until the age of two years and then becomes deaf will learn to speak perfectly, even if it did not speak before it became deaf. In the same way, the understanding and invention of abstract principles may be dependent on early influences on the still-growing brain. Something happens during the first few months after birth that molds the brain in preparation for learning, something that is lost at a later age.

Reaching out into new regions of human experience, one person may be able to grasp and put into words a new concept that others can understand when it is explained to them, but which they could not find themselves. Man is the only animal whose two halves of the brain are specialized for different tasks. The integrity of the left half is necessary for speaking a language, for reading and writing. The right half is dominant in spatial tasks, such as geometry, and probably in the formation and understanding of some of the most profound concepts. If both halves of his brain are intact, a person can use the left half to express the understandings of his right; if both sides are unequally developed, however, he may either be eloquent without expressing any concepts related to spatial understanding, or he may be unable to express his insights.

The difference between the ability to understand a concept and to express it, and its relation to the evolution of the human brain, can best be exemplified by the behavior of a person with brain damage involving the frontal lobes, the part of the brain that evolved most recently and that projects intended action onto a screen of imagination to be corrected before real action occurs. One case report relates that when such a person was asked to draw a square, she would, again and again, draw only an O, recognize her mistake, and try to change the drawing. But no matter how hard she tried, she could only make an O laboriously over and over again, never managing to produce corners. Obviously, her brain was incapable of the visual imagination that normally produces the mental model that is copied when pen is actually set to paper. When the brain is damaged, the ability to recognize something may thus be retained while the ability to produce it is lost.

In the same way, it is probable that during the evolution of the brain the ability to understand either visual imagery or abstract thought preceded the ability to express it. At any time during history or prehistory, unusually gifted individuals, able to express a new thought for the first time, may thus have found others able to understand it. Before that first thought was expressed, however, vast capacities to feel and to think differently than before may have existed, unused because ignition through a suitable intuition or explanation was lacking. The same may be true today.

Self-realization, the expression of one's individual talents, has long been realized as the most satisfying experience any person can have, provided his basic needs are fulfilled. Such an experience can be intensified if it contributes simultaneously to the well-being of other people. Strong, one-sided talents are rare. Most apparent narrowness of interests is the result of selective ridicule or encouragement, by parents or peers, of a good innate assortment of gifts. Talents do not have to be restricted to superior intelligence or originality. The simplest occupation, as long as it enhances the quality of life and satisfies the person involved, is valuable and should be treated as such. Man needs to be proud of himself. That need can be observed at every age in history and in every culture. It underlies the courage of the hero as well as the courage of the criminal, the readiness for sacrifice as well as the desire for money. All society has to do is give man a good reason to be proud.

Who is society? It is not the majority of voters, nor the sum of the persons contained in a community. Most people are easily influenced by the most vocal, most convincing expressions of a few opinions. Single individuals, as long as they think within the range of the humanly possible, may be liberators of previously suppressed and often unrealized aspirations within man's nature, expressing in words for the first time what was only vaguely felt before. If that happens, the reaction is a sway of values in the whole community, a sway that establishes itself securely after some period of struggle. The quality of a society is determined by the quality of those of its members who dare to speak.

HUMAN VALUES

The earth is a sphere floating in space on which life, man, and his values have appeared by chance. As long as men with high ethical principles could, when persecuted, retreat into uninhabited regions, values were maintained. But now the earth is filled, and every increase in population will lead to increasingly fierce and ruthless competition. If humanity can be preserved, it will only be through conscious awareness of its uniqueness, worth, and vulnerability.

The search for joy and the avoidance of pain are shared by man with every living creature that is capable of subjective emotion: man alone experiences the joys and sorrows of others.

Neither fire, nor tools, nor language made man human—but his ability to feel concern for his fellow creatures. To speak, to think, to invent, man's brain must have grown to sufficient size throughout a period of prolonged youth and helplessness. In mammals, maternal instincts are determined through hormonal activity during lactation; in man, a new mental attitude must have led to the rejection of the impulse to harm a creature just because it is weak or sick. However, compassion must have competed constantly with the striving for power forced on man by his struggle for existence. Each defeat of compassion led to a relapse into insensitivity, each victory to a new spurt of resourcefulness and imagination. Resourcefulness, in turn, eased the struggle for survival and made compassionate actions more acceptable.

Concern with compassion may seem unimportant in comparison with the ideal of freedom. Yet without internalized guidelines of fairness, freedom ceases to be. It ceases to be not only where a sense of fairness is absent, but also where its expression is prevented. Wherever well-founded outrage against single individuals is discouraged, dynamite is accumulated for mass-explosions. These may lead to such horrible additional injustices that the restoration of order by authority is greeted with relief. The worst occurs when well-founded outrage is suppressed with enough efficiency to increase the magnitude of injustice until it forces individuals to choose between insanity or insensitivity. The result is complete dehumanization.

The need for release of well-founded outrage in single instances may lead to the demand for complete animal freedom. But is an animal free? Does nature permit freedom to a creature without reason or foresight? In every lower animal, sexual intercourse is limited to a restricted breeding season or to some days of female receptivity. The lioness is the slave of her instinct to gorge herself, even if her cub dies of starvation. The compulsive compassion of the African hunting dog would lead to the death of the entire group, including the most capable hunters, should the habit of begging for food ever outweigh the hunting instinct in too many animals. Among primates, young animals are bitten to death if they do not display gestures of servility toward their superiors. The transition from instinct-bound animal behavior to the freedom of man leads over fierce, rigid, and cruel taboos. Concern for man demands his liberation from unnecessary restrictions, but it also demands a constant and careful evaluation of the results of altered guidelines for action.

Freedom is possible only where instincts have weakened far enough to permit decision-making, and decision-making depends upon interior guidelines. Man's ability to suppress detrimental impulses with the help of his foresight and reasoning power has permitted a multitude of instincts to survive, far beyond the ones needed in any one particular environment; his ability to communicate, to learn, and to remember has, in addition, permitted him to draw on the help of his ancestors' wisdom to deal with situations where his own reasoning power may be insufficient. The advocate of giving untrammelled expression to all impulses, even those that damage another person, cannot be surprised if the impulse to kill the offender is also allowed to reign freely. Granted that such a state of affairs would finally lead to the elimination of all damaging desires, no one is prepared to accept the amount of suffering involved nor the resulting constraints on behavior that would make a group viable only within a restricted environment. An animal is guided safely through most situations it meets by a balance of countervailing instincts, but it cannot survive in unusual circumstances. Survival during confrontation with unaccustomed dangers depends on the capacity for conscious decision-making, a capacity bought only at the expense of forsaking reliance on instinct.

Wherever conditions remain unchanged for a long time, traditional values guide man's actions as safely as instincts—but they are not instincts. Confronted by new conditions, man can, and has to, resort to his reasoning ability. Ninety-nine percent of all species have become extinct because they overspecialized to fit into an environment that later changed. The rigidity of the blackcap's instincts does not permit her to feed her starving young unless it directs its open beak toward her. The bird cannot think. But man can think—and he must. He can neither live without interior guidelines, nor with too rigid ones; and he must remember that his survival depended upon several reevaluations of his ethics in the past.

Man would be better able to identify his problems and see their solutions if he were unrestricted. But every person is imprisoned within his nation, his religion, his political system, or his social class. Even if he struggles to free himself from these influences, he is seen by others as belonging to a certain category and he is persecuted for crimes that others in his category have committed, often decades or centuries before his birth. Progress in ethics depends on the separation of individuals from categories and upon the separation of good ideas from an otherwise neglected context.

It is not important to believe in the story of creation as told by the teachers and prophets of the past, but it is important that questions were asked and answered which were unrelated to material needs, and it is important that causal explanations were attempted. We must be inspired by these great men, but not paralyzed. We must learn to think, not as they thought, but as they would think if they lived with us today, with our fears and with our knowledge. Sacred are not their words but their intentions.

Man must find courage to judge principles, not according to the strength of their roots in tradition, but according to their influence on the well-being of the individual. Increasing communication among all parts of the earth makes it impossible to avoid friction between different sets of values. Hunger and sickness are no longer seen as the products of fate but as caused by human indifference, while logic is nevertheless rejected as repulsive. Yet it is logic that would lead to relief. Logic, however, is not incompatible with a high regard for such values as simplicity, peace of mind, enjoyment of sensual pleasure, and appreciation of nature's beauty. Values have to be separated from their context and judged singly. Important is not their origin but their effect.

The number of people able to live on the earth depends on its size, the expected living standard, and the available level of human intelligence. The size of the earth is fixed. The expectation of a living standard that includes at least the basic necessities for a healthy and satisfying life but rejects incessant demands for extravagant luxuries is a matter of common sense. The fund of available human intelligence depends on its concern with justice. Intelligence is retained and cultivated in regions where injustices are remedied by insight; it is destroyed where they are remedied by violence.

Rejection of all ethical guidelines might uncover in many individuals contradicting desires of similar strength which, because of their interference with the decision-making process, would lead to insanity. It might release inhuman passions of sufficient strength to magnify the horrors that occurred under Hitler and Stalin. Never at any time in history could man have discarded values and continued to live; but least of all at the present stage of technological development. We cannot return to the past, but we can use our reason and insight to understand that both the warmth of the human heart *and* objective knowledge are irreplaceable treasures and that the preservation of each depends upon that of the other. Without such insight, we may pass for centuries through a deep valley of inhumanity from which we may never be able to emerge again.

Conversely, the study of human nature may find that in our society a considerable number of irrational cravings are caused or magnified by wrong conditioning and learning, while positive potentials are suppressed. Many persons may suffer from an unfulfilled longing for that kind of satisfaction that results from success after strenuous struggle. Many may suffer from a longing for meaning in life, a subjective experience that results from the convergence of self-fulfillment with the fulfillment of the needs of others. They may not know how to choose the most rewarding of their talents. Needs like these, if discovered, would lead to an unexpected blossoming of humanity.

The diversity of human values, their origins in different environments, and the natural attachment of each person to his tradition must be understood and respected. However, the possibility of mutual extermination through the most dangerous weapons ever invented makes it necessary to find a common core that is able to attract every person on earth. Core values cannot include the acknowledgment of superior nations, political systems, or religions; but they must include a high regard for trustworthiness in dealings between individuals, power groups, and countries. They cannot demand an equal division of power, regardless of talent and character, but they must demand respect and reward for positive efforts of even the smallest capacities. Their aim should be not the mistreatment of innocent persons—not even by victims of injustice—but the advance of justice and fairness on earth.

If confidence in such values as integrity and decency can be restored, the remarkable ability of man to learn can be used to his advantage. That ability may not be limitless. Man may function best under conditions not too far removed from those under which he evolved, yet neither are his boundaries known nor finite. Whatever limits may be discovered in human nature, there will always be the unexpected, the new, the evolving mind, the man who is capable of being more human than anyone before, of expanding humanity into different directions never before anticipated. Nobody knows which nation will produce that man. Even if the contributions of one or two ethnic communities are more appreciated by society in general than the contributions of others, a few generations may completely reverse that status. For that to happen, it is only necessary that all values, especially those of dependability, trustworthiness, and scientific honesty, become drastically curtailed in one society, while in another these values gain significantly in importance. Intelligent and concerned persons in the first society will then become frustrated, discouraged, silent, and fearful of ridicule and persecution. In the second society, such persons, even if their number is smaller, will achieve miracles through their gift of encouraging the best in the nature of their people. Such reversals have repeatedly occurred in history, and they are—to a certain extent—something to look forward to. Although it is deeply painful to witness the decline of a society or nation one has been taught to love, it is infinitely more painful to witness the disappearance of principles and guidelines from the earth that are indispensable for the continuation of humanity.

FACING REALITY

We have only tapped a very small part of the knowledge that is potentially available to man. If the search for reality can be carried out thoroughly enough and far enough, the present antagonism between science and ethics will disappear.

From a purely objective point of view, human values are a peculiar absurdity in the universe. From a subjective point of view, they are the most sublime treasure in the world, for which even the sacrifice of our lives is justified. The subjective view was for many thousands of years a co-determinant of human action and, as such, an effective agent in evolution. That they are not of extraworldly origin but correlated with—and probably the result of—the emergence of our nervous system does not destroy human values; it elevates them to their legitimate place in the struggle for survival. Realism cannot exclude recognition of the power emanating from the evolution of ethics in man, and no reason in the world forces us to relinquish that power now.

Our question cannot be: "What is more important, the survival of the human species, or our desire to be just and good?" It must be: "How can we ensure the survival of the desire to be just and good?"

Any urgent need may awake the dormant capacities of an individual and induce him to advance a small step into a formerly unexplored region. The excitement produced by such an event will attract many capable minds into that field, and a spurt of growth will suddenly occur where advancement seemed hopeless before.

Until now, the destruction of enemy nations was perceived as the most urgent need in any one country. The concentration of brilliant minds on this task, however, has produced such effective weapons that further success in that direction would now be identical with self-destruction. As a result, a paralysis has set in, a paralysis that encourages the spread of uninhibited torture and inhuman practices by organized power groups. The preservation of human values is the most urgent need at present.

Traditional wisdom alone is not sufficient.

Love and compassion have been preached for centuries in the West, but corruption and organized crime are spreading through its cities.

Love and compassion have been preached for centuries in the East, but several hundred thousand people are living and often dying in the streets of Calcutta.

Love is not enough.

Compassion is not enough.

Feeling one with all mankind is not enough.

All revolutions and many wars and mass killings are desperate attempts to remedy injustices, but nearly always the original motives are submerged in the intoxicating vision of unlimited power, and, together with some criminals, the best-intentioned, the most upright, the most gifted persons are killed.

Hatred, deceit, and violence can never lead to the creation of justice; they lead to nothing but its destruction.

The only possible approach toward justice is through *a combination of love and concern with reason and insight*.

Such a combination opens the eyes to the existence of three immense barriers that impede our efforts to solve present problems:

1. The belief, prevalent in religion, that extra-human powers care for the fate of man.
2. The belief, prevalent in science, that man's survival is independent of ethical guidelines.
3. The fear, constantly deepening the chasm between science and ethics, that objective knowledge destroys human values.

Again and again the question is asked: "If no God exists, why should we be good?"

It can be answered: "Because we are human, because we are proud to be human and do not want anything less."

But God exists.

He exists, as long as he is recognized as an expression of the highest human aspirations, as an expression of man's longing for a merging of love and reason into one, for a merging of those powers which are at present so fatally divided.

CHAPTER SIX

The Magnetism of an Encompassing Vision

The American Psychological Association's annual convention was slated for Los Angeles in August 1994. At the previous year's meeting, held in Toronto, Roger Sperry had received the APA's Outstanding Lifetime Contribution Award, the field's highest honor. Unfortunately, Sperry's deteriorating health—he suffered from the degenerative nerve disorder ALS, also known as Lou Gehrig's disease—prevented him from travelling from his home in Pasadena to Toronto to accept the award, which in his absence was presented to his son Ted. But it occurred to Antonio Puente, past chairman of the APA, that despite Sperry's worsening condition the 1994 convention would be close enough to Pasadena to make feasible the idea of a "last tribute" with the Nobel laureate himself attending. Sperry's students and collaborators were invited from all over the world to report on their work, and a social get-together was planned at Caltech's Atheneum at Pasadena, which Sperry promised to attend. It was, alas, a promise he could not keep: he died on 17 April 1994. The gathering was held in his memory, and Erdmann wrote "The Magnetism of an Encompassing Vision" to be presented there. As she was unable to travel to Los Angeles, Dr. Polly Henninger read the paper in her absence.

MY ATTRACTION TO SPERRY'S WORK AND THOUGHT

Perhaps I am the only person, or at least the first, who was attracted to work with Dr. Sperry not because of his outstanding achievements in science, but because of his refusal to let these achievements dominate and limit his world view.

My first encounter with Sperry's visionary thinking occurred through reading "Bridging Science and Values" (1979). In that article, he expressed with convincing power the belief that in a sound and healthy world facts cannot be pursued at the expense of values, and values cannot be pursued at the expense of facts.

Here, I read from the pen of a neuroscientist—an *outstanding* neuroscientist—that values, not electrochemical activity, or synaptic transmissions, or action potentials, but *values* determine our actions and decisions. Of course, Sperry knew very well that all this physical sparkling inside our braincases is essential and he never dreamed of neglecting its importance; but he also knew that we could not function unless all this fire was first translated into subjective experience, and that it is our own special subjective experience that allows us to think and that makes life worthwhile and meaningful.

When he first expressed these views in the mid-sixties, they seemed heretical. In 1979, when I read them, they were halfway on their route to acceptance, and now in the nineties they are taken for granted. Even an authority in neuroscience such as Gerald Edelman now maintains that "consciousness is efficacious."

But it was not Sperry's mind-brain theory that carried me away. It was the extension of his quest from *how* we think to *what* we think, and to the way in which our thinking affects the quality of human life on earth and the long-range prospects of our biosphere. In Sperry's view, that step was natural:

> Within the brain we pass conceptually in a hierarchical continuum from the brain's subnuclear particles, on up through the atoms, molecules, and brain cells to the level of nerve circuit systems without consciousness, and finally to cerebral processes with consciousness. Objective facts and subjective values become parts of the same universe of discourse. . . . The scientific image of man regains much of the freedom, dignity, and other humanistic attributes of which it long has been deprived.

In other passages, the image of our creator is reinstated, brought closer to reality, and described as being of awe-inspiring grandeur.

All of this, I felt, was written from *my* heart. Of course, I dreamt of assisting Dr. Sperry with his work, and I was elated when my dream came true. Not that everything went smoothly; on the contrary, to say that I "helped" Dr. Sperry would be a euphemism. In fact, I managed to make his life more difficult by disagreeing with many of his most cherished convictions. Our greatest bone of contention was "competition." Sperry felt that evolution knows best, that our brains, our thoughts and our spirituality were the result of the struggle for survival in nature, and that we would still be crawling around like earthworms or slime molds, were it not for competition.

I was appalled by the waste of genius I discovered in the scientific papers I had to read in the library during my tenure as Sperry's research assistant. How much highly valuable time was misused to diminish the impact of an opponent's contributions! Nor was I convinced that evolution's creation and subsequent elimination of 99% of all species in existence displayed wisdom of a superior kind—a wisdom we ought to copy. I would draw pictures of an evolutionary tree with all branches clipped off due to extinction, and only a feeble shoot making it up to the top, and Sperry would draw innumerable sideshoots and offshoots on the surviving branch, supplying nature with the wonderful variety of life he loves so much. –Needless to say, after nine years of these debates and discussions, each of us was more than ever convinced of our respective position's validity.

Nevertheless, for me the time was immensely fruitful. I conducted, independently, a research project, "In Search of Values for Human Survival," and, as a result, came to publish *Humankind Advancing*, a quarterly dedicated to the promotion of more far-sighted, responsible attitudes. I also published *Beyond a World Divided*, a book on Sperry's thought and philosophy for the general public, written together with a science writer, David Stover. This book concentrates on Sperry's courage, on his advance, again and again after each victory, into new and unexplored territory, alone, attacked by his critics, and overcoming all obstacles, drawn forward by his encompassing vision.

For me, too, it was his vision that overpowered all disagreements and that was the reason for my staying on until I was convinced I could be of no more use to him. He never asked me to leave.

SPERRY'S SUCCESSIVE ADVANCES INTO NEW AND UNEXPLORED TERRITORY

Beyond a World Divided introduces Sperry this way:

> Roger Sperry looks at human problems from a larger perspective, one that brings into focus not only all of mankind but all of life—and beyond that, all of creation. From this vantage point he sees humanity as a small but extraordinary fragment of reality, endowed with the gift of mind—probably the most amazing product of evolution—but wasting that gift and, indeed, on the verge of destroying it. Sperry sees warring world views defending facts against ideals or ideals against facts as part of a larger whole, as incomplete fractions of the same reality. . . . [That] reality is ruthlessly eliminating all unrealistic expectations (that is, expectations that fail to take account of nature's laws) while at the same time condemning to subhuman conditions those without *any* expectations, ideals, or values. In Sperry's view, "unrealistic expectations" are created not only by belief in supernatural powers, but also by unwarranted confidence in the ability of materialistic, reductionistic science to compensate for the loss of such beliefs.

Earlier in his life, Sperry was drawn by lure of the mind-brain problem first toward the investigation of brain development, work which he himself tended to look back on as more radical and more basic than the later split-brain research, and in which he invented the experimental paradigms that people have used for the last thirty years. Having succeeded, however, he reacted to his victory in an unexpected way. While eager researchers crowded into the field he had opened, he preferred the challenge—and the loneliness—of asking new questions and being the first in a new area.

This new field, his split-brain research, the work for which he received the Nobel Prize, had an immense impact globally, not only in the world of science but also among the general population. —Yet even all this glory failed to keep him permanently within the boundaries of his chosen domain.

At the height of his success, Sperry reacted in a fashion intensely typical of his character: he stepped forward beyond all his previous work to accept the challenge of a far greater, more difficult, and more important task. He even went so far as to call all his previous efforts "relatively minor in their implications" compared to his present concern with consciousness, ethics, and values. Transcending traditional boundaries of science, he advanced into philosophy.

Crucial to Sperry's philosophy are the concepts of emergence and downward causation—the appearance of new phenomena and laws through first-time constellations of atoms and molecules in the universe, and the causal effect of these phenomena and laws on all previous (as well as subsequent) evolution. These causal effects disappear—and with them any adequate representation of reality—with the dissection of entities into parts.

Contemplating ethics, Sperry turned to the wonders of nature as pole star. For him, the "forward thrust of evolution" was an awe-inspiring phenomenon that it was wrong to destroy and degrade, and right to enhance and revere. He often corrected me when I spoke of "human survival" and maintained that survival alone can occur under degrading conditions; what we have to aim for is "quality survival."

THE REORIENTATION OF HUMANITY TOWARD QUALITY SURVIVAL IN A SUSTAINABLE WORLD

How can "quality survival" be achieved? A new more encompassing vision is needed to attract humankind away from short-sighted, solely money-oriented interpretations of success to true advance—advance that liberates hidden, and largely unknown, potentials within the human brain.

Concerned and farsighted thinkers agree that if we continue to equate success with immediate material gain, we are in danger of creating a small, irresponsible, and unconcerned upper class, taking advantage of the vast majority of human beings who live in abject misery—and whose proliferation would be encouraged, because it will increase the size of the market for material goods. That mass, of course, would be kept gullible, uncritical, and in such desperation that they would sell everything they have, even their health and their morals.

Alarm about this development leads to a counter-reaction that infuses ethical values enshrined in ancient traditions with new life. Ethnic coherence is defended to the extreme. Even supraethnic values, such as Catholicism, are guarded with new tenacity. As late as 1993, contraception was declared a sin by Pope John Paul II in what was described in *Time* magazine as "perhaps the most important document of his papacy."

Both magnets, the one of money and its counterpart, the one of guidelines opposed to science, are pulling humanity back to conditions comparable to those experienced in the Middle Ages, or worse.

In the face of these powerful determinants of human decision-making, the new magnet of an encompassing vision, so beautifully described by Sperry and so well reinforced by his integration of science and values, provides a beacon of hope for our future that can hardly be overrated:

> In the eyes of science, to put it simply, man's creator becomes the vast interwoven fabric of all evolving nature, a tremendously complex concept that includes all the immutable and emergent forces of cosmic causation that control everything from high-energy subnuclear particles to galaxies, not forgetting the causal properties that govern brains and behavior at individual and social levels. For all these science has gradually become our accepted authority, offering a cosmic scheme that renders most others simplistic in comparison and which grows and evolves as science advances.

This emphasis on constant enrichment of our view of reality, on constant increase of our understanding of nature, including human nature, and on the need for a constant re-evaluation of our guidelines is, I believe, the most mature and promising attitude to which we can aspire. Only now do I see clearly why I feel so uncomfortable with an overemphasis on competition. Competition, whether in nature or culture, leads to advantages only within the *present* situation. Competitive advantages, when the situation changes, turn into disadvantages. Human beings, who are able of foresight—or at least a glimmer of foresight—have the right and the duty to transcend the limitations of non-human nature.

A NEW DEFINITION OF "THE HIGHEST GOOD"

A new definition of the highest good is suggested as a goal for our species to strive for: the capability of foresight and insight. Long-range foresight is a prerequisite for quality survival on our planet. The new goal would not contradict Sperry's demand to revere and enhance the forward thrust of evolution, but would help to focus and direct it. —If that new ideal could be substituted for the present money-God that threatens to destroy our species and our earth, reasons for a counter-reaction would be absent, our efforts to regulate population growth would be much more successful, and we could look toward the future with renewed hope.

Though diverging somewhat from the definition given by Sperry, the above suggestion is fully in line with his thinking. Nor is it incompatible with a tribute to him. On the contrary, it highlights one of his qualities which, though occasionally mentioned, has not yet been sufficiently appreciated: the ability to provide an atmosphere that encourages in his co-workers critical thinking, self-reliance, and creativity.

I am firmly convinced that, if the grand vision Sperry described becomes the pole for our new mental compass, the recognition of his work and his impact will grow with each century to come.

CHAPTER SEVEN

Roger Sperry and the Search for a Science of Values

In both Beyond a World Divided *and* A Mind for Tomorrow, *Erika and I wrote at length about how Roger Sperry's work on consciousness, with its consequent implications for the relationship between science and human values, might in time lead to a more extended conception of science, and, perhaps, a way of approaching values in a scientific fashion. I recall a letter from Erika in which she expressed qualms about describing Sperry's work as a "search" for a science of values. Roger Sperry was too much the objective scientist (she said) to ever "search" for a specific, preordained goal: he went where the facts led him. Nonetheless she let the phrase stand, both in the title of one of the chapters of* A Mind for Tomorrow *and in the following essay, written by the two of us in the late 1980s and sold to a small-press magazine called* Hobson's Choice, *which, alas, ceased publication before the piece could appear.*

"In the last century no one has contributed more to our understanding of the development and cognitive functions of the brain than Roger W. Sperry." So declared Princeton psychologist Charles G. Gross in a recent issue of *Science.* But Sperry's influence extends beyond science itself. In Gross's view, no psychologist since Freud and no biologist since Darwin have done more to change the shape of popular culture.

But who is Roger Sperry and why are his ideas regarded so highly by his colleagues? Now professor emeritus at the California Institute of Technology, Sperry won a half-share in the 1981 Nobel Prize in medicine and physiology. He is best known for what is called his "split-brain" work—studies which demonstrated the dramatic difference between the thinking methods of the human brain's left and right hemispheres.

And yet, despite the influence his ideas have had both on the scientific study of the brain and on the wider world, Roger Sperry would scarcely be considered a household name among non-scientists—a curious anomaly in an era of superstar scientists who write bestsellers and host television series.

Why is that? There are various reasons. Most important, perhaps, is Sperry's long-held conviction that, in the end, ideas matter, not fleeting celebrity or popular acclaim. Driven by a concern that those ideas be properly and accurately expressed, he has hesitated to present them in a more popular, accessible form. He seldom grants interviews and invariably turns down invitations to appear on radio or TV. It's not that his personal appearance would detract from the impact of his thoughts. On the contrary—he is an impressive and charismatic man. But for years he has battled primary lateral sclerosis, a slowly progressing paralysis that is irreversible. This condition, which also affects his speech, tends to worsen when he is excited or under stress, which of course would be the case during public appearances. As a result, Sperry prefers solitude. He often takes vacations in isolated retreats where he can be at one with nature. Such retreats also seem to greatly improve his health and hold back the spread of the paralysis—a condition, we should emphasize, that does not impair the mind, but, paradoxically, seems to sharpen it and to expand the scope of his thinking.

This is the intensely private man whom Gross compares to Darwin and Freud. Think about that comparison for a moment. Darwin did more than overhaul biological theory; he changed forever the way we think about the living world. And Freud transformed the way we think about ourselves. Having just finished a book dealing with one aspect of Sperry's work, we think Gross hasn't exaggerated his importance. Sperry's research could change our world just as profoundly as Darwin's or Freud's.

Roger Sperry has spent most of his life inside the human brain—figuratively, anyway. He spent the first two-thirds of his career establishing fundamental new insights into how the brain functions and how it deals with the outside world. In the final third of his career—the period after many people would have taken "early retirement" and gone off to the golf course!—Sperry has taken on an even greater challenge: the age-old puzzle of how mind and brain are related. Part and parcel of that research is a radically different view of how science can help develop a coherent, useful system of human values.

Sperry's work on science and values—his "search for a science of values," if you like, though Sperry insists he is searching for nothing but the truth of how the world works—has met both compliments and controversy. But that has been true of his scientific career since the beginning. For more than 40 years he has thought to unravel the secrets of mind and brain. Interestingly enough, that journey began in a university English department—

Any young man or woman who has started down one track, whether in school or the work force, only to consider abandoning it and pursuing another interest, can find some reassurance in Sperry's career. A road can have a few twists and turns and still get you to your destination. In 1935, at the age of 22, Sperry graduated from Oberlin College with a bachelor's degree in English literature. Sperry would probably have made a good English professor: he has that precision of phrase and fastidiousness for revision that are often the hallmark of the breed. Indeed, the authors of this article can testify to his unstinting demands for accuracy of both style and substance. And it isn't just a quality he demands of others—he holds himself to the same high standards, revising his papers interminably to get the prose just right.

English literature's loss was science's gain, however. After finishing his B.A., Sperry switched majors, to psychology for his M.A. and to zoology for his Ph.D., each time attracted by the secrets of brain function. Ironically, though, he would come full circle four decades later, as he tried to find a way reconciling science and the humanities. In fact, he went so far as to declare that in some ways scholars in the humanities had been right all along, and scientists had been mistaken.

This wouldn't be the last time Sperry would make abrupt course changes in his academic career. What interests him is not filling in the details after a new discovery has been made—a task which can be more than adequately accomplished by the great numbers of young scientists who immediately flock to the scene. Instead, it's the adventure of going forward into uncharted territory, alone, that excites Sperry—and which has kept him busy practising science well into his seventies.

Before striking off on a new course, however, Sperry made significant, even seminal contributions to not one but two areas of study in the field of physiological psychology—the understanding of brain function and its effects.

Let's go about this chronologically. Following Sperry from Oberlin, where he earned his master's degree, to the University of Chicago, we see him studying for his Ph.D. in the laboratory of Paul Weiss, one of the best-known neuroscientists of the period. Under investigation is the question of how the body's nervous system is "wired up." At that time (during the 1930s and 1940s) the view prevailed that nerves would function the same no matter how they were hooked up. They were thought of as unspecified, lifeless, inert—much like electrical wiring. Plug your TV into this outlet or that, it doesn't matter; as long as the proper type of current is provided, the TV set will work.

But that is not the way the body operates. Nerves are pre-programmed to accomplish specific tasks, and it *does* matter how they are connected.

Now, wait a minute, you will say. That's true of our homes too. Household washers use 220-volt current, while other lights and appliances use 115-volt current. Isn't the outlet we use for the washer, then, in a sense, "pre-programmed" for that function? We certainly could not plug a TV set using 115-volt current into the washer's outlet without very dire consequences for the TV set.

In fact, there seems a certain similarity—at least up to a point. Still, nerves behave quite differently from household wiring, for they are alive. As they develop, they actively grow—push themselves forward among a tangle of other nerves—toward specific goals they are destined to connect with. How do they do it? How do they know? —These problems, only partly perceived at the time, filled the atmosphere in Weiss's laboratory with tension and suspense.

The most striking thing about Sperry's discovery was that it directly contradicted the work of his doctoral supervisor. Paul Weiss had been carrying out experiments which had upheld the previous theory—that nerves can be switched from one task to another, and that their original "wiring" pattern does not matter. Weiss proposed what became known as the "resonance theory": that nerves can be tuned in certain ways, rather like way in which you can tune a TV set to a particular channel.

Sperry's experiments, however, showed that the exact opposite was the case. Nerve cells (or neurons) cannot switch channels. Even when fairly young, Sperry—and this is the hallmark of a genius—never blindly believed what someone else had "proved," even if that someone was his supervisor.

The rigor of his logic and his investigations now led to a rivalry of two choices: did genes determine the ultimate connections that were established, or was experience the decisive factor? It was thought the nerve cells might somehow learn through trial and error what their functions were to be while the fetus was developing.

(It's worth noting in passing that the entire history of evolution is a story of learning through trial and error, with the punishment for error being death and the elimination of any descendants. If a creature made a mistake, the result was simple: no more of this exact kind of creature ever again. If, on the other hand, the creature—without reasoning and by chance—acted correctly, its genes transmitted detailed instructions for its replication. —Only when through this brutal trial-and-error learning a most interesting novelty, nerve cells—and with them memory—appeared for the first time on earth could inevitable fatality be avoided. Errors would still be made, but not invariably repeated, as animals were able to build successfully on their experiences. And in time, even this kind of trial-and-error learning appeared primitive as evolution produced something more sophisticated yet: human beings' ability to use reason and imagination to project how various situations would turn out, and, ideally, avoid errors altogether.)

But back to Sperry. We now join him as he experiments with newts, or small salamanders, trying to trace the source of neural "knowledge." In the first set of experiments, he rotates a newt's eyeball, turning it through a half-circle. The result is that, when an insect comes into sight, the newt jumps in the opposite direction. His world is turned upside down!

No amount of experience changes the newt's behavior, and Sperry concludes that genetic pre-programming—not learning—is responsible for the way nerve cells are connected.

But how? Could experiments be devised that would show directly how the nerves connect themselves? This time, Sperry not only rotated the newt's eyeball but severed its optic nerve as well. While healing, the nerve fibers fight their way through a virtual no-man's land of scarred and broken tissue—and, amazingly, manage to hook themselves up precisely and correctly to the nerves of the retina. No compensation, however, is made for the fact that the eyeball had been rotated—the programming occurs according to a standard procedure, blindly, automatically.

What determines that goal-directed regrowth? Obviously, it does not follow a particular channel or conduit, since the optic nerves find their way to the appropriate connections without any such guidance. Instead, Sperry suggested, each nerve cell has a chemical tag or marker, and these markers can be used to tell one nerve cell from another. Using the analogy of electric wiring, it's as if each wire is coded with a particular color and set of numbers, so that an electrician would know enough to hook up red wire #234A to blue wire #234B. But in the case of nerves, of course, there is no outside electrician—the nerves recognize each other. As Sperry himself explained it, "the outgrowing fibers are guided by a kind of probing chemical touch system that leads them along exact pathways in an enormously intricate guidance program that involves millions and perhaps billions of different chemically distinct brain cells."

And who installed this fantastic wiring program? Professor Mary Midgley of Newcastle upon Tyne in England says it most succinctly: "Evolution did."

Sperry's "chemoaffinity theory," as his nerve-connection hypothesis came to be called, has been generally accepted for half a century. It proved clearly superior to the resonance theory of Sperry's supervisor, Paul Weiss. Worldwide, scientists are occupied exploring the details of how actual linkages are made at the level of individual molecules. But the validity of the principle itself is irrefutable. Viktor Hamburger, Sperry's long-time colleague, calls it "one of the few general unifying principles in today's developmental neurobiology."

Far from being satisfied with his success, however, the young scientist tackled another important problem. Having earned his Ph.D., he moved on to post-doctoral work under the supervision of Karl Lashley, who was well known at the time through his theory of "cortical equipotentiality." That theory holds that each part of the brain's cortex can adapt itself to any task that comes along. Again, Sperry challenged and disproved his mentor's theory. "I know of nobody else," Hamburger remarked, "who has disposed of cherished ideas of both his doctoral and his postdoctoral sponsor, both at their time the acknowledged leaders in their fields."

It might have been easy for Sperry, having made these important discoveries, to spend the rest of his career exploring them in greater detail. What, for instance, was the molecular basis of chemoaffinity? —He chose another path. By the early 1950s Sperry had launched into the investigations which would find the widest popular interest and which would later lead him beyond science into philosophy and the humanities. This was his work on the twofold nature of the human brain.

The brain is divided into two hemispheres, connected by a "bridge" of about 200 million nerve fibers, the corpus collosum. One of the great mysteries facing neuroscientists in the 1940s and 1950s was the nature of this "bridge." There were reports that cutting it completely caused no effect. Theories abounded about the purpose of this huge bundle of nerve fibers, including one suggestion by Sperry's supervisor, Karl Lashley—perhaps only half joking—that the corpus callosum was something like a support beam, designed to keep the two halves of the brain from sagging too much.

This was the enigma that attracted Sperry and his students, first in Chicago and about two years later at the California Institute of Technology, where it dominated their research. By carrying out experiments on cats and monkeys, they were able to reverse previous conclusions and give us a dramatic new insight into the workings of the brain.

Sperry and his researchers found that "brain bisection"—severing the corpus callosum altogether—resulted in each hemisphere operating completely on its own. It was as if two brains or conscious minds existed inside one skull. The two sides of the brain perceived the world, remembered information, and carried out tasks independently, with one side unaware of what the other was doing! Bisection of the brain even led to the ability to perform two different—and contradictory—tasks at the same time.

Research on animals could only reveal so much, of course. What were the effects of brain bisection on human beings? That question was answered in the early 1960s, when two Los Angeles-based surgeons, Joseph Bogen and Philip Vogel, carried out operations called "commissurotomies." These operations were intended to provide relief for patients who suffered from epileptic seizures, and the surgeons proved successful in their aim. With human "split brain" patients now available, it was possible to study how each hemisphere was related to the higher mental faculties.

The result of studies showing that the left hemisphere dominated in such areas as writing, speech, and mathematical calculation had been anticipated because of previous observations of patients who had suffered brain damage in accidents. Surprising, and utterly unexpected, however, was the discovery that the right hemisphere made special contributions to human awareness. It excelled in such things as music, visual tasks, and tasks involving the grasp of spatial relationships.

In fact, Sperry and his colleagues were able to show that far from being an unimportant partner of the left hemisphere, the right hemisphere possessed a consciousness of its own—but one far different from the left hemisphere's primarily verbal, analytical approach to the world. The corpus callosum, far from being an inert bridge holding up the two sides of the brain, is a tremendously active "artery" of information flowing from one side of the brain to the other.

Neurologist Antonio R. Damasio has called the discoveries by Sperry and his collaborators nothing less than "revolutionary." And like many revolutions, this one quickly spread beyond the confines of its original homeland—science—into the world at large. The theory that the left hemisphere was the home of analytical methods of thought, while the right hemisphere was the source of holistic, integrating ways of thinking, became general knowledge so quickly and yet so firmly that it seemed as if it had always been taken for granted. Many popularizers carried the contrast one step further: the left brain, with its cold, analytical approach, was seen as the source of the relentlessly expanding technology which threatened both the environment and traditional ways of life; while the right brain with its holistic approach, was seen as a source of hope for a kinder, gentler, greener future.

Other writers tried to apply knowledge of the differences between the brain's two hemispheres to more personal concerns. Recently a book was published suggesting how a better understanding of a person's right hemisphere could improve personal relationships. —As with many other discoveries, the fire of enthusiasm led to wild speculations, misunderstandings, and exaggerated expectations. In fact, one of the authors, after mentioning her work with Sperry, was seriously asked by a young artist: "How can I knock my left brain out?"

Though Sperry himself always insisted on the need for a balance between the hemispheres and never indulged in fantastic projections, we think it's fair to say that some of the popularizations have drawn far too many tenuous conclusions unsupported by the evidence. But it can't be denied that Sperry's research revealed something profound about the way we perceive the world and think about it. The powerful pull all of us feel at times between rationality and emotion, between cool analysis of a situation and a quick, intuitive reaction, between the need to verbalize and deep "knowings" which defy words—this pull is mirrored in, and indeed created by, the very structure of our brains. As the Nobel Prize committee declared in making its award to Sperry, his work has "provided us with an insight into the inner world of the brain which hitherto has almost been hidden from us."

Yet the man so honored was to leave the exploration of that "hidden world" to others. For Roger Sperry it was time to change course again, to address an even more basic question: Just what is consciousness, anyway?

Until the 1960s, psychology had been dominated by a 50-year period of behaviorism, a theory which held that observing overt behavior alone, and how that behavior related to the stimulus which initiated it, was all that was objectively possible, and—most importantly—all that mattered. We could never know what was actually going on in another person's mind; therefore the concept of "mind" should be eliminated from the vocabulary of psychology, together with everything related to it—feelings, values, convictions, and so on. Replacing them would be a new and scientifically valid concept, the stimulus-response relationship.

Through this new approach, it was thought, it would finally be possible to mould human behavior successfully. Carefully modifying the stimuli which human beings encountered would lead to corresponding changes in their responses—that is, their behavior. Then, once we understood human behavior well enough, massive social engineering projects could be carried out, which would result in virtual Utopias. Indeed, one of the leading behaviorists, B. F. Skinner, projected just this sort of behaviorist heaven-on-earth in his novel *Walden Two*. In another book, *Beyond Freedom and Dignity*, he argued that such traditional concepts as "freedom" had no meaning within the behaviorist worldview. If it were to advance, humanity would have to abandon such obsolete notions and adopt the behaviorist program.

If the behaviorists were right, then the traditional world of the humanities—the world of myth and literature, not to mention the everyday world of human emotion as expressed in casual conversation—was nothing more than a mirage. Human thought, if it existed at all, was irrelevant; everything could be explained in terms of stimulus and response, cause and effect. As J. J. C. Smart put it, "living organisms, including human beings, are simply very complicated physico-chemical mechanisms."

Despite its success—and behaviorism was a successful theory in many ways, for it explained many issues which had previously remained unclear—the behaviorist position never won unanimous approval and was, even while it dominated, perceived as thoroughly unsatisfactory by many people, both within science and outside it. Psychologist Sigmund Koch spoke from the heart—and voiced the fears of many of his contemporaries when in 1964 he deplored the fact that behaviorists had translated "every mentalist category distinguished in the history of thought, including . . . the medieval scholars" in terms of stimulus and response. Under such a view, Koch warned, psychology might become a "mass dehumanization process."

In spite of this general, and increasing, dissatisfaction with behaviorism, no viable alternative could be found.

Sperry himself, like most young scientists, had at first been quite impressed by the breath of fresh air that a scientific approach to behavior promised, and that a stale, boring, and unsuccessful introspective psychology sorely needed. But his habit of thinking thoroughly led him to reject the notion that the mind was an unnecessary concept. In the early 1950s, he published a paper in which he declared that "real understanding" of the link between the mind and brain "could have vast influences on all the ultimate aims and values of mankind." Then, during a conference in 1958, he expressed for the first time the logic that would later, fleshed out in a series of scientific papers, lay the foundation for overturning behaviorism and re-establishing the mind as a factor that mattered in psychology.

"A good case can be made," he argued at that 1958 conference, "for the contention that in most or all conditioning, the stimuli used, in order to be effective, *must register as sensation or feeling in the neural stream of subjective awareness.* [Emphasis ours]. In other words the animal must feel the pain from the shock, must smell or taste the meat juice, and so on. . . . Any physiological model of the conditioned response that fails to include the subjective properties is . . . bound to end up with some kind of gap in the chain of cerebral events." —All his later papers elaborated on this basic and convincing argument made during a meeting dominated by behaviorists.

The conclusion to be drawn was obvious. If subjective experience is important in animal conditioning, how can it be thought unnecessary in understanding human beings?

The essential points underlying Sperry's new world view are deceptively simple:

(1) Consciousness emerges from brain activity.

(2) Consciousness must be understood as what it is, at its own level—in other words as subjective experience, as thoughts, emotions, and ideas—not as the underlying activity of brain cells.

(3) Matter is controlled by mind.

Let's consider these points in greater detail, starting with the first: Consciousness emerges from brain activity.

The behaviorists dismissed consciousness as irrelevant. On the other hand, people who hold traditional Christian beliefs argue that the world of matter and the world of spirit are two fundamentally different things. The essence of a human being, they say, lies in the possession of an eternal soul that is purely spiritual.

Sperry's view cuts halfway between these two extremes; it combines the most valid elements of each worldview. Like most scientists, he believes that the world can be explained through the working out of various natural laws and processes. There is no evidence for a separate, spiritual realm which exists apart from matter. On the other hand, he believes that consciousness is more than just brain activity.

Here we must pause to explain a fundamental phenomenon of nature: *emergence.* It's not an overstatement to say that emergence is one of the most remarkable aspects of reality, valid throughout the universe, and the driving force behind evolution. Emergence occurs whenever a combination of parts creates a new whole, a new entity with properties and laws that have never existed before. The nature of the new properties and laws is determined not so much by the parts themselves as by their specific organization—their relationship with one another. The novelty of the emergent item is a quality of the whole alone. The parts themselves don't possess it, nor do they possess just a bit of it. Ice, for instance, is created by a specific lattice-arrangement of water molecules, which these assume when the temperature falls below 32 degrees Fahrenheit. It makes no sense to speak of a single water molecule freezing.

Emergents can either be material objects or subjective mental experiences, created by the unimaginably complex interactions of nerve activity in the brain. That is the belief Sperry holds, and that's why he is convinced a separate realm of the spirit is unnecessary. A deeper understanding of the worldview of science permits us to accept subjective experiences as part of a one-world reality system. But such experiences appeared in the universe only after complex brains had evolved; a single neuron can't be conscious.

The second major element of Sperry's worldview—that consciousness must be understood as what it is, at its own level—follows from the first point. If we try to reduce consciousness to its individual parts, it disappears. The content of our thoughts simply cannot be understood in terms of the electrical and chemical interactions of brain cells, though it depends on them. Consider a television set. In order to receive a TV program, the set must be in good working order. But the actual content of the television program you're watching—the storyline of a drama, the jokes in a comedy series, the content of a news broadcast—cannot be explained no matter how much you know about the transistors or tubes within the TV set. To be sure, when Sperry uses the TV-analogy, as he often does, he always points out that while television sets receive their programming from outside—that is, from a TV station—brains are able to program themselves. In brains, the images elicited through experience and memory are powerful enough to create new subjective experiences, which again are creatively active. For this reason Sperry insists that interaction within the brain must be understood as occurring at a higher level than that which we understand through the study of neurons alone.

Finally, we come to the last element of Sperry's view of mind and brain—that matter is controlled by the mind. This, again, follows from what we've talked about so far. While the subjective experiences created in the brain interact with other experiences, arouse desirable or detrimental images of the consequences of intended actions, and finally lead to a decision, these events are constantly accompanied by brain activity occurring at the same time. Sperry believes that specific decisions cannot be made, and the appropriate activity of the neurons cannot be initiated, unless such conscious deliberations occur. In effect, those conscious experiences act as "programmers," just as the signal transmitted by the TV station controls what we see on the screen. Physiologists call the movements of our muscles and limbs "motor activity." This activity is controlled by certain types of nerve cells called "motor neurons." Both motor activity and the discharging of these motor neurons are material events; but both are controlled by and depend upon mental activity beforehand. We think before we act; and thus matter is controlled by mind. (This course of action refers only to the voluntary nervous system, of course. A large part of motor activity, such as heartbeat, respiration, or digestion, is involuntary, and is automatically controlled by the brain without the involvement of consciousness.)

Such an understanding of the mind-brain relationship is incompatible with the behaviorist, materialistic point of view which claims that everything—including intentional human behavior—can be fully explained in mechanical, materialistic terms. In contrast, Sperry points out that we act the way we do not because we are mechanical, stimulus-response robots, but because we are thinking, feeling beings whose brains can make sense of the world. Far from excluding science, such a viewpoint, Sperry emphasizes, asks that science take account of the way the world really is. We cannot distort reality, or discard aspects of it, just because they are too complex to fit into the oversimplified framework that our present state of science can conveniently explain. (Just think what our view of reality would be like if we restricted ourselves to what we knew 100 years, 500 years, or several thousand years ago!) Consciousness does exist; it can't be reduced to the flickering electro-chemical charges of brain activity. In fact, the nature of consciousness is a legitimate area for scientific inquiry—not something to be ignored.

Sperry expressed this point of view for the first time in writing in 1964, and continued to elaborate on it in subsequent papers. —A decade later, he discovered that the entire field of psychology had changed tremendously. A "consciousness revolution" or "cognitive revolution" had swept through the field, and the behavioral sciences abounded with discussion of, and research reports about, the nature of consciousness—a topic that had been taboo only 10 years earlier.

Not everyone agrees with Sperry's view, of course. There is plenty of criticism. Especially controversial is Sperry's claim that scientific facts and human values are compatible—that statements about what is can tell us what we ought to do. Most philosophers disagree vehemently. And, too, behaviorism, while on the wane, still represents an important force in the psychological community.

On the other hand, Sperry's ideas have won considerable support, sometimes from surprising quarters. Engineer E. M. Dewan has pointed out that non-material emergent properties, the same kind Sperry noted in the case of consciousness, can also be observed in non-living systems. Electrical power generators, for instance, will tend to oscillate at slightly different speeds when isolated. But when hooked together into a single power network, they fall into step. The system as a whole displays properties which none of the generators, standing alone, possesses. Engineers call such a regulator, which is not located in any one place, a "virtual governor." On a vastly more complex scale, something of the same kind occurs when consciousness emerges from the workings of billions of brain cells. We call it "the mind."

Other support comes from the humanities. English professor M. E. Grenander, for instance, says Sperry's work possesses "overwhelming significance." And, indeed, Sperry's ideas suggest that in some ways, at least, artists, writers, and humanists have been right all along: thoughts and emotions do have a real existence and they can affect the world. —He believes that if we illuminate values with facts, and facts with values, we would move a long way toward a saner, safer future.

Consider the world of the late twentieth century. In many ways it is a world poised at the edge of the abyss. We are threatened by environmental collapse, by runaway population growth, by a persistent inability to resolve our problems peacefully.

If trends persist, our very civilization could be destroyed within the next century.

According to Sperry, the problems facing the world have a common denominator: "While man has been acquiring new, almost godlike powers of control over nature, he has continued to wield these same powers with a relatively shortsighted, most ungodlike set of values, rooted, on the one hand, in outdated biologic hangovers from evolution in the Stone Age, and, on the other, in various mythologies and ideologies."

Unchanging values in a changing world seriously threaten the survival of our species, Sperry believes. To stem the rush of global disaster and to build a better world, the same method that led to the meteoric rise of science—critical analysis and the constant comparison of theories with facts—must be extended to values.

Sperry is not alone. Among others, Jonas Salk, inventor of the polio vaccine bearing his name, is also concerned with this pressing issue. Underlying such efforts is the conviction that the old tradition of an "objective" science—a science removed from considerations of values or ethics—is no longer viable. Unless scientists find some way to apply their knowledge to ethical questions, humanity—and science with it—may very well cease to exist.

It has always been Sperry's habit to look at evolving reality from a larger perspective. Human beings were created by the forces of nature acting over billions of years. We are part of the "grand design of nature" that includes the entire biosphere. Its fate is our fate; and scientific fact and human values alike drive us to find solutions which will preserve that fragile biosphere in all its diversity, including our striving toward human dignity and freedom.

Roger Sperry's entire life has been a quest for truth, starting with his concentration on the brain. His first major area of study involved the basic nerve connections which allow us to sense and act in the world: how they are formed and how they function. In the second phase of his career, he examined the very different ways in which the two sides of the brain perceive the world. In the last phase he has taken on the even more fundamental problem of how mind and brain are related, and how science can help us make decisions about human values.

Like many quests, Sperry's seems destined to remain unfinished. But his contributions to science have been enormous, and his stature seems likely only to grow, as other scientists carry on, in the decades ahead, the search for the mysteries of the human brain and for a science of values that he began.

CHAPTER EIGHT

Voyage into Uncharted Waters

The following essay was written by Erdmann in 1998 at the request of the Foundation for the Future, and was also subsequently published in Humankind Advancing. *In it, she touched once again on the concepts of emergence and downward causation, but perhaps the most noteworthy element is the call for the creation of a "new profession of 'intermediaries'—persons able to understand the core principles of two or more specialized fields and translate them into each other."*

I must go down to the seas again, to the lonely sea and the sky,
And all I ask is a tall ship and a star to steer her by . . .

—John Masefield, "Sea Fever"

When the Phoenicians or the Vikings took off into the wide open sea, their main driving force was the thrill of exploring the unknown. But without the patience, knowledge, and reliability of competent ship builders, they would have perished. Nor could they have ventured far from their shores without the skill of star-guided navigation.

The possibilities inherent in ongoing evolution are vastly greater and more wonderful than our imagination can conceive; and yet the depths and dangers ahead may end our voyage shortly after leaving the shore. —How can we build ships, safe enough to carry us forward into an unknown future? —How can we find the right stars to guide us?

Ever since human thinking expanded beyond immediate necessities, questions have been asked about the origin of the world, and answered in accordance with the best knowledge available at any given time. Animals or their spirits, the wind or the sun, were deified and received offerings to secure their favour and protection; they shared the cravings and shortcomings of mere mortals—even when they were elevated to gods in human shapes ruling from Mount Olympus in ancient Greece. It was a large advance in mental maturity when God was conceived of as a single superhuman reality, the incarnation of absolute justice, wisdom and benevolence—an ideal that no human being could reach but toward which all of humanity must strive. How far-sighted that conception was is being realized only now, thousands of years later.

We now know that God is not a separate entity, but a construct of our mind. Without this construct, this ideal, however, humanity would have destroyed itself. Conceived of as an external authority whose laws cannot change, God himself becomes destructive; he prevents desperately needed ethical adjustments to a changing biosphere. Conceived of as a useless fiction to be discarded, he will leave a void that acts like a magnet, attracting confusion and irresponsibility. But conceived of as the product of the finest minds on earth, as an eternal part of those who passed away, of their urging to search for the best in us and our world as they did in theirs, he becomes a star that guides us on our voyage through uncharted waters.

The safety of our voyage ahead depends upon constant co-evolution of knowledge and values.

THE SHIP OF WELL-ESTABLISHED KNOWLEDGE

During a discussion after his guest-lecture at the California Institute of Technology about a decade ago, Nobel laureate James Watson, the co-discoverer of the intricate structure of the DNA molecule, was asked by a young listener: "If you were a student entering university today, trying to decide on a field in which you had the greatest chance to make fundamental discoveries, discoveries with the impact of those you have made, which field would you choose?"

"The brain—how we think," Watson answered at once.

The speed and conviction of the answer was even more impressive than its substance. Watson apparently spoke about something that had occupied his own thought for a long time.

And why is the brain of such importance? Because our human future and the future of our earth depend upon its performance. More knowledge about how we think, and why we think as we do, may prevent hopeless efforts in the solution of our problems that would lead only into dead ends. It may shed light on how to find more adaptive ways of thinking, and how to achieve genuine progress toward a desirable and sustainable quality of life.

Therefore, the evolution of the brain will receive a disproportionate amount of attention in the following summary of core principles inherent in evolution.

CORE CONCEPTS OF EVOLUTION

Evolution is the consequence of the flow of energy, the ultimate origin of which is shrouded in mystery. Occurring at first by chance alone, evolution gradually displayed increasingly lawful behavior, as chance-created events and formations assumed guiding functions of their own. But chance is never absent, and the future cannot be predicted, even if full knowledge of the past could be achieved. The dramatic story of the cosmos, its emergence from a highly condensed energy source, the appearance of galaxies, stars and planets in the turbulence of its energy flow, the production of ever more complex atoms during successive star creations and explosions, the bonding of atoms to form chains of diverse molecules, and finally, the advent of self-replicating super-molecules surrounded by protective cell walls—the evolution of life from inorganic matter—has been told in detail in nearly every biology textbook and is constantly being refined by eminent scientists [1, 2]. Thus, this paper will be restricted to the discussion of only the drama's core concepts.

Emergence and Downward Causation. Everything is energy, although the semi-permanent interlocking of specific counteracting energy forces is perceived as matter by our brains. When two or more atoms, molecules, or constellations of molecules combine, a completely new entity is created. Properties and qualities of the constituent entities disappear, and new properties and qualities come into being. Such a process is called emergence. When it happens for the first time during the process of evolution, something is created that never existed before.

For instance, two hydrogen atoms and one oxygen atom, both gases, will combine into water. The qualities of water, and its effects on previously evolved entities, are fundamentally different from those of the elements that brought it into being. Water, but not its gaseous constituents, can carve canyons into rocks, collect in ocean basins, and provide an environment for early life to flourish. The effect of newly evolved entities on previous evolution is an example of downward causation.

There is nothing extra-worldly about the change of properties in chemical combinations, nothing that is not inherent in all matter. No mysteries are involved, except the one great mystery: the existence of energy; the existence of the tendency to act. The properties of a congregation of atoms or molecules in the gaseous stage result from an increase in speed of their vibrations, which leaves no time for the weaker cohesive forces to become effective, as they are in a liquid or solid. The latter differs from the former again only by the degree of its constituents' independence. In a liquid, cohesive bonds are not strong enough to resist attempts of exterior gravity to separate them, in a solid they are. Other properties, like color or texture, are based on the reflection or absorption of portions of the light spectrum or on the particular arrangement of atoms in a solid. All properties are the result of different relations of energy.

Matter itself is an emergent property of energy. Subatomic events do not have to be matter to create matter, nor do atoms have to be alive to create life. Similar, only of infinitely more complexity and more impact, are the changes that led from living matter to conscious experience. There is no point where the mind enters the body, just as there is no point where life enters into non-living chemicals [3].

The rejection of these thoughts is based on the common misconception that mind is therefore degraded to matter. That is not the case. Matter is one manifestation of energy, consciousness is another one. Neurons in the living brain are not conscious. They are the substructure and framework facilitating, organizing, and guiding billions of constantly changing energy interactions, which we subjectively experience as thoughts and emotions.

Cosmic, biological, and cultural evolution are the effects of constantly ongoing emergence and downward causation—of continuous changes in energy relationships, continuous creation of new phenomena, and continuous effects of these phenomena as wholes upon previously evolved nature. It was water, not hydrogen and oxygen in separation, that provided the medium for early life to flourish; it was a living organism, not its separate atoms and molecules, that first moved forward in a preferred direction, which led to the increase in size and complexity of the front ganglium (neuronal complex) and the development of the brain, and it was the interaction of billions of energy constellations in the brain that gave rise to conscious thought, the most powerful phenomenon affecting our world at present.

While the concept of emergence was understood and used by science for over hundred years, the concept of downward causation was neglected and even ridiculed as anti-scientific until a few decades ago. Consciousness, the most fascinating and powerful part of brain activity, was considered a useless side effect. Values did not count. As a result, life was flat and meaningless, unless refuge was found in supernatural beliefs. All this changed about thirty years ago, when neuroscientist and Nobel laureate R.W. Sperry elevated downward causation to a concept of greatest importance in brain function, dedicating all of his later life to its explanation and that of its consequences [4, 5, 6]. First vigorously rejected, the insight that consciousness is causal is now widely accepted in science [7].

Consciousness is subjective experience of energy interaction, translated into meaningful information by the brain. We don't see billions of sparks flitting about, we see flowers and trees and we experience their beauty—we see the sun set beyond the horizon and we experience a sense of elation. This translation, and it alone, enables us to direct energy interaction in the brain deliberately.

The Evolution of Purpose and Meaning. The most common misconception about evolving nature is that our lives are meaningless and without purpose, unless purpose preceded, and guides, evolution. Like consciousness, however, purpose and meaning are results of billions of years of chance interactions, which gradually became constrained and directed by new emergents. That does not detract from their significance. On the contrary: as creations of evolution, our inner experiences of freedom and responsibility co-determine the further flow of evolution and infuse our existence with a new and deeper meaning [8].

Conscious purpose evolved as a result of forward movement in one direction. Single-celled organisms without neurons move in random directions, initiated by changes in the membrane due to outside agents, e.g., light rays or olfactory chemicals, which induce course reversal when a region of optimum living conditions is left. In multicellular organisms, cell specialization led to preferential survival and reproduction of creatures with nerve cells, with ganglia (nerve centers) along the back and with coordinating interneurons. Forward movement led to concentration of special sense receptors in the front ganglion, or the head.

During the passage of millions of years, ever more specialized neuronal centers developed and pushed the old ones aside. These did not disappear or become inactive, however. Ancient reflexes are still active to avoid damage to eyes or limbs before the association cortex is consulted and thought occurs. Of importance, too, remains the early autonomous nervous system, which, without conscious input, regulates such vital functions as breathing, heartbeat, and digestion, and which remains active even during sleep or anesthesia. The next step in brain development, decision making in the limbic system, determined by interacting hormones and sense impressions, likewise still acts independently if the neocortex (new cortex) is impaired, e.g., by drugs or alcohol. But before this impressive center of reasoning arrived on the scene, an older structure took its place, which integrated sense input and regulated muscle activity. That old cortex, now pushed toward the back of the brain and called the cerebellum, is also still actively involved in its original function, which proceeds without conscious input. The entire brain is a conglomerate of task-specialized units, each of which evolved millions of years apart in response to then prevalent conditions, and all of which affect one another [9].

Conscious choice, purposive activity, decision making, and thought arose with the growth of the neocortex, which acquired deep inward folds to gain more space. The most remarkable and latest addition, however, the prefrontal cortex, evolved only 100,000 years ago. That structure, with vital connections to the neocortex (the reasoning center) and the hormone-regulating limbic system in the interior of the head (the center for emotion), functions as the seat of social sensitivity, foresight, and long-range planning. This latter ability is found in one of the latest evolved convolutions, the lateral sulcus principalis [10]. It is surprising that the prefrontal cortex does not affect intelligence [11]. The superiority that is measured by IQ tests is not the same as the wisdom we most urgently need. Without a functioning prefrontal cortex, the necessity to care for the fate of our earth and the fate of future generations cannot even be perceived.

The entire evolution of the brain was accompanied by a perfection of learning and memory, which involves changes of neuronal firing that intercept and reroute innate stimulus-response sequences. That did not happen without a price: An animal in its natural habitat is attuned to its environment. It can act according to its impulses and at the same time do what is best for its survival and that of its species; all detrimental instincts have been eliminated by the death of their bearers. Only where learning has advanced to such overwhelming importance as in the human species, only where detrimental impulses can be suppressed while its bearer lives and reproduces, only there is a separation between desired action and right action possible [12]. If both coincide, however, life achieves a special glow.

The source of that inner glow may lie in the care for those one loves, in the feeling of being one with nature, or in the perfection and use of a special gift. The most distinctively human source is creativity.

Creativity cannot be forced into being. It takes place below the level of consciousness, but only if a problem has been thoroughly worked through at the conscious level. Often, an inventor wakes up at night with the solution to a puzzle that had evaded him or her for weeks—or a new insight occurs during preoccupation with another task. It seems that subconscious wrestling with a difficulty permits chance-interconnections of thoughts, which streamlined logic prohibits. For the same reason, uninitiated outsiders, or newcomers to a field, can often find a solution that is invisible to professionals with life-long experience. Not all inspirations are solutions, of course. Evaluation by experts and controlled tests help to discover errors.

Also, even if creativity cannot be forced, it can be facilitated, for instance by what Edward De Bono calls "lateral thinking." Instead of pursuing a problem in a linear fashion, it is put aside and then attacked again from a different direction [13]. The same happens when worldviews and cultures clash, or when we recognize that we have entered a terra incognita—a situation that never before occurred on earth.

For creativity to proliferate and become a desirable part of our culture, it was first necessary to loosen rules and regulations enough to accept new thoughts, but not so much as to lead to the collapse of society. A standard of ethics had to be developed and constantly updated to take new knowledge into account. In short, a science-value co-evolution had to be initiated upon the conscious continuation of which our species depends.

OUR GUIDING STARS

During another influential lecture at the California Institute of Technology, a place that produced an unusual number of Nobel laureates in spite of its small size, Aron Kupperman, professor of chemical physics, stunned his audience by exclaiming that "intelligence is the most dangerous product of evolution!"

He argued that brains have evolved through fierce competition; they incorporate the urge for fierce competition. They have to, otherwise they would not have succeeded in their development. —All life is competitive, but especially animal life. As the ability for photosynthesis was lost, as amino acids had to be taken from other living things, normal competition turned into a fierceness that steadily increased. The invention of ever more potent weapons may make the self-destruction of any intelligent, technologically competent life unavoidable—not only here on earth, but on any planet anywhere in the universe. Self-destruction at our stage of civilization may be the law of the universe [14].

The Cosmic Principle of Self-Destruction. Many scientists are well acquainted with the "cosmic principle of self-destruction," though not all share Kupperman's conviction that we are abandoned to a fate beyond our control. For instance, the space scientist Eric Chaisson grants that mutual destruction could result from "a drive toward complexity that effectively runs out of control," an accelerating rate of change that eventually exceeds the capacity of the human brain to handle it. For those who believe this, he says, the universe will never progress beyond the present "matter-dominated" stage. His own thinking, in contrast, includes the hope that minds somewhere in the cosmos, "though not necessarily here on earth," may acquire the wisdom to circumvent such a threatening fate. His suggested solution is to "adopt cosmic evolution as a guiding paradigm and nouveau scientific philosophy for our time, which requires us to think in dynamic rather than static terms, to forge a link between natural science and human history, to realize the evolutionary roots of human values, to renew a sense of hope" [15]. —As history shows, the consequences of thinking in static terms are disastrous.

The Fate of the Easter Islanders. Just as instinct-directed organisms disappeared, entire civilizations vanished when their rigid guidelines were not changed in response to changing environmental conditions. Such was, for instance, the fate of the Easter-Islanders, as reported by Duane Elgin: "With a mild climate and rich, volcanic soil, Easter Island was a paradise covered by forests and filled with diverse animal and plant life when it was first settled by Polynesian colonists in approximately 500 A.D. As the Islanders prospered, their numbers grew to 7,000 or more, and they used the resources of the island beyond its regenerative capacity. Archeological evidence shows that the destruction of the forests on Easter Island was well underway by the year 800—about 300 years after people first arrived. By the 1500s, the forests and palm trees had disappeared as people cleared land for agriculture, and used the remaining trees to build ocean-going canoes, burn as firewood and build homes."

Jared Diamond, professor of medicine at UCLA, describes how the animal life was eradicated: "The destruction of the island's animals was as extreme as that of the forest: without exception, every species of native land bird became extinct. Even shellfish were overexploited, until people had to settle for small sea snails. . . . Porpoise bones disappeared abruptly from the garbage heaps around 1500; no one could harpoon porpoises anymore, since the trees used for constructing the big seagoing canoes no longer existed . . . " [16].

"The biosphere was so devastated that it was beyond short-term recovery. With the forests gone, ocean fishing no longer possible, and animals hunted to extinction, people turned on one another. Centralized authority broke down, and the island descended into chaos with rival groups living in caves and competing with one another for survival." Eventually, according to Diamond, the islanders "turned to the largest remaining meat source available: humans, whose bones became common in late Easter Island garbage heaps. Oral traditions of the islanders are ripe with cannibalism." By 1700, the population had crashed to between one-quarter and one-tenth of its former level. When the island was visited by a Dutch explorer in 1722 (on Easter Sunday), "he found it [says Elgin] a wasteland almost completely devoid of vegetation and animals" [17].

Apparently, no one on the island thought of population control and resource preservation (as was done on other Polynesian islands), or these solutions were disregarded and their promoters expelled. Instead, an inordinate amount of ingenuity, work, and effort was expended to build huge stone statues, probably in expectation of relief due to their metaphysical powers. It was not spirituality that was missing, it was its link to empirical evidence. Duane Elgin calls this behavior of the Easter Islanders "collective madness" and compares it with the present behavior of Western industrial civilization, encouraged by the mass media, which denudes the earth of resources in the vain hope of finding satisfaction, happiness, and meaning in the accumulation of unneeded material possessions.

Islands of Sanity. It was Jonas Salk, the discoverer of the Salk vaccine for polio, who suggested building "islands of sanity" in this ocean of collective madness. These would consist of persons with extraordinary wisdom and insight who protect each other against destructive forces from the outside. He envisioned the merging of such islands into continents of constructive positive attitudes, leading to a predominance of sane and healthy thinking on Earth [18].

Islands of sanity are now being built everywhere; my quarterly *Humankind Advancing* is dedicated to the search for, and promotion of, the work of persons with the gift to lead our species toward greater maturity. Space limitations prohibit the mention of even a small fraction of the remarkable work I have discovered—but I must make one exception: It is the thinking of Dr. Robert Muller, who encountered the darkest sides of human nature during the war and during his thirty years of service for the United Nations without ever losing hope and confidence in humankind's potential, who invented and implemented a new system of education, starting during early infancy, that implants the realization of being a part of the cosmos and of being responsible for the planet into a child before local history is taught, and who is an irrepressible wellspring of new ideas [19]. It was he who entrusted me with vital and fascinating work for our future.

Taming Complexity. That work led to new insights. An inherent drive of evolution either toward more love or toward more competition is questionable; a drive toward more complexity is not. That drive, as Chaisson warns, may run out of control. As our knowledge grows with breathless speed, specialization will proliferate and mutually incomprehensible worldviews and languages will increasingly clash with one another, leading to ever more ferocious conflicts. How can we tame complexity?

As brains became more complex, interneurons evolved which transported sense inputs from different sources into the association cortex for adequate decision making. Similarly, inputs from different special fields must be combined into a new overarching network through which more farsighted, future-oriented choices of action become visible. We need "intermediaries," persons able to understand the basic principles, language, and world views of two or more specialties, and to make them comprehensible to one another.

In addition, new standards of excellence are needed as we proceed forward. Instead of categorizing persons according to their IQ, it will become necessary to ask whether their conduct is conducive to the generation of an atmosphere of fairness.

The Challenge. About 3.9 billion years ago, all then-existing life was nearly poisoned by the evolution of photosynthesis and oxygen accumulation in the atmosphere, until organisms were "invented" which used oxygen in their life cycles. That solution did not merely rescue life on earth, it caused an unprecedented proliferation and diversification of life, that ultimately led to the emergence of intelligence.

Now, intelligence itself threatens to poison our biosphere unless the small flickers of wisdom and foresight appearing here and there on earth are condensed and allowed to grow. These flickers are, in comparison with other determinants of human behavior, presently so insignificant that many highly capable scientists are unable to see them at all. Kupperman, for instance, argued that our only salvation was to go into outer space and search for advanced intelligence elsewhere in the universe. "If we can find only one single civilization in the universe more advanced than ours—only a single one among possibly millions—then we would know that survival is possible" [20].

Conversely, the struggle for power in nature has become invisible to a large number of well-meaning individuals, who decry its presence in humankind as an aberration that occurred only during the last centuries of our history and is rooted in reason. Reverse history, they demand, reverse evolution, and start all over again with a time of blissful harmony between human beings and nature. —That would not help, however, even if it could be done, because a state of blissful harmony never existed. Paradise, like God, is an ideal to strive for. The struggle for power is part of nature. Though symbiosis and co-operation are also important elements, as notable biologists and evolutionists point out [21, 22], they do not eliminate the struggle for power, they make it more successful. Whether at the level of atoms, cells, organisms, or nations, unification leads to competitive advantage.

But it is not necessary to deny that competition was an important factor in evolution to arrive at the insight that, in the presence of increasing intelligence, further single-minded concentration on this aspect would be fatal to human and other life on earth. —To change course, not the rejection of science and reason is required, but the full understanding of the concepts of emergence and downward causation, the fact that later evolved phenomena influence the course of previous evolution.

Reason is lethal only if it remains the servant of the struggle for power; as soon as it becomes its master, reason will be our savior.

Knowledge, responsibility, wisdom (which is reason combined with love), these are the building materials we need to carry the sails of our exhilaration and creativity. —Our guiding stars are our ideals, which we cannot see if we rely on reason alone, and which we cannot reach if we abandon reason.

END THOUGHTS

Consciousness led to insight into the waste and cruelty of blind progress, and, in spite of its amazing results, prohibits continuation of its methods. Evolution took two hundred million years—each year generating, testing, and discarding innumerable evolved cell types—until finally two prokaryotes were compatible enough to work together. The results were dramatic: their symbiosis produced the first eukaryote, which contained an organizing device that made all subsequent evolution vastly more efficient [23]. Can similar progress be achieved with more humane and less wasteful methods? I believe, it can—if evolution of the subjective experience of freedom is understood as a new causal determinant in our world, and if responsibility is merged with courage.

Well-informed but fearless, standing in the bow of a storm-tossed vessel, with the hand firmly gripping the wheel and the mind alert, the venturer into the unknown is inspired by a sacred conviction: Even if competition is an integral part of evolution, even if it threatens to destroy all technologically advanced civilizations, even if it has already done so on other planets, and left the cosmos void of life—even if the cosmic principle of self-destruction is the law of the universe—I will not despair.

I will steer our ship toward yet undiscovered shores of wisdom!

I will prove the law of the universe wrong!

CONCLUSION

1. *The survival and further advance of our species depends upon conscious science-value co-evolution.*

2. *We have to develop a new profession of "intermediaries," persons able to understand the core principles, viewpoints, and language of two or more specialized fields and translate them into each other.*

The most important ethical requirement to cope with increasing factual details, however, is trustworthiness. At one point in the future, even the most proficient translator will be unable to understand more than a small part of our growing knowledge. At that time, unless we can trust one another and know that our knowledge is being used for the common good, the cosmic principle of self-destruction will become effective.

REFERENCES AND ACKNOWLEDGEMENTS

I wish to thank Duane Elgin, the Fetzer Institute, and Eric Chaisson for permission to quote from their work, and David Stover for reading the paper and making valuable suggestions.

[1] De Duve, C. *Vital Dust: Life as a Cosmic Imperative*. New York: Basic Books, 1995.

[2] Swimme, B. and Berry, T. *The Universe Story*. London: Penguin Books, 1992.

[3] Erdmann, E. *Realism and Human Values*. New York: Vantage, 1978.

[4] Sperry, R.W. "An objective approach to subjective experience: Further explanation of a hypothesis." *Psychological Review* 77 (1970), 585-590.

[5] Sperry, R.W. "Holding course amid shifting paradigms." W. Harman and J. Clark, eds., *New Metaphysical Foundations of Modern Science*, pp. 99-124. Sausalito, Calif.: Institute of Noetic Sciences, 1994.
[6] Erdmann, E. and Stover, D. *Beyond a World Divided.* Boston: Shambhala, 1991.
[7] Edelman, G. *The Remembered Present.* New York: Basic Books, 1998.
[8] Erdmann, E., 1978, op. cit.
[9] Wise, R.A. Notes from Lectures in Physiological Psychology, Sir George Williams University, Montreal, 1969-1970.
[10] Erdmann, E. "Neural Substrates of Planning and Voluntary Activity." Unpublished term paper for Psychology 413, Sir George Williams University, 1970. Supervisor: Professor Jane Stewart.
[11] Warren, J.M. and K. Ackert, eds. *The Frontal Granular Cortex and Behavior.* New York: McGraw-Hill, 1964.
[12] Erdmann, E., 1978, op. cit.
[13] De Bono, E. *Future Positive.* New York: Penguin Books, 1979.
[14] Kupperman, A. "Cosmology—The Origin of Life, Evolution, and Religion." Lecture at the California Institute of Technology, 12 February 1987.
[15] Chaisson, E. "Our Cosmic Heritage," *Zygon* 23 (1988), 409-479.
[16] Diamond, J. "Easter's End," *Discover*, August 1995, p. 68.
[17] Elgin, D. *Collective Consciousness and Cultural Healing. A Report to the Fetzer Institute.* Millennium Project, P.O.Box 2449, San Anselmo, CA 94960.
[18] Salk, J. "The New Epoch," P. Weintraub, ed., *The Omni Interviews*, pp. 95-115. New York: Ticknor and Fields, 1984.
[19] Muller, R. *Ideas and Dreams for a Better World.* Santa Barbara, Calif.: Media 21, 1997.
[20] Kupperman, A., op. cit.
[21] Margulis, L. "Symbiosis and the evolution of the cell," *Yearbook of Science and the Future.* Encyclopedia Britannica, Inc., 1982, pp. 104-122.
[22] Laszlo, E. *Evolution: The General Theory.* Cresskill, N.J.: Hampton Press, 1996.
[23] Mayr, E. "The Probability of Extraterrestrial Intelligent Life," in E. Mayr, ed., *Toward a New Philosophy of Biology.* Cambridge: Harvard University Press, 1988, pp. 67-74.

CHAPTER NINE

Pro-Reason, Pro-Nature, Pro-Humanity: Struggling Toward a Viable Worldview

Much of Erdmann's work was concerned with ways of reconciling science and religion; that, in fact, was the primary theme of Beyond a World Divided. *Unlike such prominent, outspoken atheists as Richard Dawkins and Christopher Hitchens, Erika felt that there remained a place for religion in the modern world, despite the fact that the cosmologies underlying such faiths as Christianity, Judaism, or Islam had long since been superseded by a scientifically informed understanding of the universe's properties, evolution, and origins. The following brief piece was written for the newsletter of the Institute for Religion in an Age of Science (IRAS).*

On the pre-scientific level, we are often ourselves destroyed, eliminated with our false theories; we perish with our false theories. On the scientific level, we systematically eliminate our false theories—we let our false theories die in our stead.

—Karl Popper

There appear to be at least three tests that can be applied—not to whether a picture of reality is correct, but to whether it appears to be a wholesome one for society to hold. These are: 1. Does the view in the long run lead toward societal or system adaptability, and hence toward survivability? 2. Does the view lead toward fruition of the long term trend of human civilization? 3. Is the view compatible with whatever can be discovered to be man's most fundamental nature?

—Willis W. Harman

The good news is that these quotes are not contradictory. The bad news is that this is not generally realized; it is widely assumed that science and reason stand in the way of ethical progress. Even Professor Loyal Rue, to whom I am deeply grateful for inviting me to write this essay, implies in his book *By the Grace of Guile* that no alternative exists between the truth of a chance-created universe without meaning and purpose and the "noble lie" of a meaningful creation story, which is needed to keep humanity on track. But an alternative exists. It is the principle of emergence at the core of evolution. The struggle toward a viable world view—or more precisely a world view that would secure a viable ecosystem, a viable humanity as part of it, and the unceasing glow of the spark within that draws us toward wisdom—should be of special relevance to IRAS members, as they are in the business of clearing away misconceptions arising between the viewpoints of science and those of religion, and doing so at the highest possible level of insight and understanding.

Among those beliefs obstructing our progress, the ones I am encountering most persistently (and not only from non-scientists) are the following:

1. Darwin was wrong.
2. The population problem is irrelevant.
3. Science is identified with materialism and greed.
4. Traditional science must be replaced with a "new science," which does not insist on verifiable (or rather falsifiable) data.
5. Understanding the interrelationship of the web of nature is a sufficient ethical guide.
6. Consciousness exists independently of a living brain.
7. Purpose or meaning cannot exist in our world unless they preceded evolution.
8. Mystical experience cannot be explained by science and therefore proves the existence of supernatural powers.
9. Drug-induced states of consciousness lead to the perception of superior truths.
10. Life is meaningless unless it continues after death.
11. Quantum mechanics proves the existence of psychic powers at a distance.
12. Heisenberg's uncertainty principle makes all scientific knowledge irrelevant.

I am burning to defend my objections to these beliefs in detail, but Loyal Rue took the precaution of restricting my essay to 1,500 words. Thus, I will simply speak of the struggle, which consists on my part in vigorous letter exchanges and the sampling of new world views to widen my horizon and look at the problem from different perspectives.

Pursuing that endeavour, I encountered fascinating papers and books, the most relevant of which was *Evolution: The General Theory* by Ervin Laszlo. That book displays a breathtaking panorama of our evolving world from the position of systems theory. According to that theory, different systems, such as the atom, the cell, the organism, societies, ecosystems, and galaxies, are at the most fundamental level guided by the same organizational principles, such that the knowledge of one of these systems leads to the understanding of all of them. This thesis has been contested on the grounds that human systems are different, because they rely on conscious intentional action. But if it is assumed that consciousness is not an emergent of the living brain, but exists in the universe at large, and that it occurs in atoms and cells as well as in the neocortex, this objection does not apply. In the organic realm, Laszlo sees a succession of subsystems, systems, and supersystems, in which each system's advance toward greater complexity is followed by a transformation, combining independent constellations into one larger one, after which the process is repeated. The organizational complexity of the larger system is at first simpler than those of its subsystems, but increases again until a new transformation takes place. In such a way, atoms, molecules, cells, organisms, etc., arise. Binding forces are strongest at the lowest level, that is, in subatomic particles, but become increasingly weaker at higher levels. At the human level immense difficulties have to be overcome to achieve cohesion. Yet, unless this evolutionary imperative is achieved, mutual annihilation will be a constant threat.

The scheme is exhilarating. It goes beyond Darwin and focuses on the role of co-operation as a major evolutionary strategy. But related reading was deeply disturbing. Concern with humaneness gave way to inordinate emphasis on the need to reject traditional rigorous science. For instance, it was demanded (not by Laszlo, but by one of his admirers) that the subjective experience of a medium, who wrote two books allegedly dictated to her by a scientist 20 years after his death (he had continued his studies in the beyond), be accepted as scientific data! And this was by no means an exception. Such demands effectively block the wholesome world view toward which we (and Laszlo) aspire. Systems and chaos theories do not conflict with science, yet they seem to attract believers in the most incredible claims. The same happened to the work of Roger Sperry, who had become the guru of the flower children of the Sixties, after his discovery that the right hemisphere specialized in intuitive, artistic thinking, and religious experience, and that it was essential for a meaningful life and functioning society. But he took care to dissociate himself constantly from claims that his discovery supported belief in the occult and supernatural. One of his several papers on the topic, "Holding Course amid Shifting Paradigms" (published posthumously), explains again his position that consciousness is an emergent of the living brain, although it affects brain function and is not an epiphenomenon.

Though the right hemisphere must supplement the left one, it cannot replace it. The expulsion of science and reason from our civilization would open a void into which ruthless and irresponsible elements would rush to feed on confusion and despair. Our acquisition of a viable world view may be likened to a caterpillar's metamorphosis into a butterfly. Within the safety of the cocoon, a complete transformation takes place, during which the entire interior dissolves and is reorganized. Everything is demolished, except for a vital part: the DNA-information that carries the instruction to create the butterfly. What is the cultural equivalent of this DNA-information, the most vital part to be preserved? I believe it is our reasoning power, together with our capacity to be humane, and the glimmer of foresight that must be encouraged to grow and replace present shortsighted and destructive policies.

The key problem is that intuitive knowledge cannot be corrected when it is in error. Belief systems based on revealed religion are therefore far more likely to fight each other until death than those containing components of reason.

But not only is the rejection of science and reason dangerous, it is also unnecessary. The most beautiful experiences in life are not erased through scientific discoveries; they are deepened. I will close with a quote from *Beyond a World Divided* in support of Sperry's contention that no life exists after death:

> There is a way in which even the devoutly religious person may transcend his concern with the unembodied self, not through the rejection of his or her belief, but through experiencing the divine at a more fundamental level, unchained from any dogma or specific belief system. During that experience the individual meets the divine in depth and in truth, becoming one with the universe. All its separate, distracting aspects vanish. It no longer matters whether the entity once known as "I"

> remains alive after death: all that matters is the overwhelming sensation of a love that knows no boundaries. The quest for the life of the individual soul after death becomes irrelevant.

Here believers in all the religions of the world, be they of the West or the East—and even those confessing no faith at all—are unified during moments of their deepest experience.

To succeed in our struggle toward a viable world view we need a more profound understanding of science and a more profound understanding of religion. I cannot think of any group better suited than the members of IRAS to lead us toward that aim.

CHAPTER TEN

Vision and Reality

"Vision and Reality" was co-authored by Erika and me in response to a call for submissions to a contributed volume entitled Evoluting, *edited by E. Todd Ellison. The project began in the mid-1990s, but the book never ended up being published, and so the essay appears here for the first time. Its argument that we must "readjust our goals and targets from chasing mirages to pursuing realistic aims" seems even more relevant today than it did then, as does the insight that, if the focus of Western civilization is to be reoriented from unlimited economic growth to personal fulfilment, the best means of generating support for such a reorientation is not by fixating on needed sacrifices but, rather, by emphasizing the positive rewards of such a shift in priorities. The world has become considerably more crowded, polluted, and despoiled since "Vision and Reality" was written almost two decades ago, despite the best efforts of the environmental movement, and one suspects that part of the reason lies in the movement's refusal to move away from a rhetoric of sacrifice, despite considerable evidence that such a strategy is not working. How I wish Erika were still with us today to put these more recent developments into context!*

If you have built castles into the air, your work need not be lost; that is where they should be. Now put the foundations under them.

—Henry David Thoreau

Humans were not built to fly, and biological selection has for eons steered us toward an exclusively terrestrial existence. Yet we started to dream of soaring, and eventually we found ways to break the bounds of gravity and realized that dream.

—Mihaly Csikszentmihalyi

Few would deny that this is the age of science. Because of science, our world has expanded both in space and time, from the medieval, human-centered cosmos no more than a few thousand miles wide and a few thousand years old, to a vast universe thousands of millions of light years across. Four hundred years ago, the planets were no more than points of light in the night sky; today we know them to be worlds as complex as our own, and our space probes whiz by orbs that were unknown to Galileo and Newton.

Science's success in unravelling the basic underpinnings of the physical universe has been nothing less than meteoric. But why has science been so successful? The answer, we think, lies in the process at the heart of science: the constant cross-checking of vision against reality, and reality against vision.

Scientists prefer to say they test hypotheses against observations, or theories against underlying facts, but we think our formulation captures the process more evocatively.

Armed with visions of how they believe the world is structured, scientists then test those visions against the reality their instruments and experiments reveal, and adjust or abandon their theories accordingly. And sometimes, too, the process works in reverse: new visions or theories of how the universe works are so compelling they lead scientists to look at the universe in an entirely different light—to make observations no one had ever thought to carry out before, and hence to reveal hitherto hidden aspects of reality.

This is how science works; and it seems to us that if a similar method could be adapted to other human endeavours—particularly in the realm of politics and society—problems that now seem intractable could be solved and roadblocks that seem insurmountable removed.

And what are the roadblocks that prevent us from solving the world's political and social dilemmas? One of the most important is the widespread belief that if human beings were to acknowledge their innate limitations, our progress would be impeded.

Quite the contrary: only by knowing our limitations can we build solid, reliable social and political structures upon them, structures built of visions and dreams and the longing for a better world that will not crumble at the first touch of reality.

And this too: only by knowing our limitations can we transcend them. Only by knowing where we fall short can we compensate for our deficiencies and build fair and just and lasting societies despite those deficiencies.

Why do we think as we do? How did our brains evolve? To what extent do the physical limitations of our brains and bodies enslave us? To what extent are we their masters? Science is now beginning to answer these questions, to hint at how our limitations are genetically determined and yet, paradoxically, how our genes have given us also the foresight and the flexibility to overcome those limitations. To get at these issues, let us go back in time, back down the evolutionary tree, and consider a brain far simpler than our own—that of an amphibian, or, to be precise, that of a frog. Imagine the little creature reacting to a moving, curved black object that it sees. The frog's motor system acts directly and immediately, jutting out its tongue. And the frog must act that way. Even if the tongue hits a sharp object instead of the expected delicious bug, it is tossed out again and again. The frog is the slave of a nervous system rigidly pre-programmed to react a certain way to particular stimuli. It has no choice in the matter.

Now let's go on to cats. Here, the decision to act on visual input is made in the cortex, several orders higher in the brain than was the case with the frog, and influenced by vast numbers of different cells at each juncture. Whereas the frog, which has no cortex, thinks directly with its retina, the cat's more complex brain permits greater acuity, versatility, and, most importantly, choice.

But the scientific study of cats led to another, much more exciting discovery: the growth of the nervous system and its interconnections is affected by experiences. What a little kitten experiences in its very first days of life—how much light each eye receives after it is opened—will determine the growth pattern of the visual system (Hubel and Wiesel, 1962). The critical period in which such changes occur lasts three to four months in kittens, one to two years in monkeys, and five to ten years in humans, the differing length of time reflecting how environmentally-dependent brain growth becomes more crucial as the brain itself grows more complex. In his Nobel lecture, Wiesel points to the probability that "other aspects of brain function, such as language, complex perceptual tasks, learning, memory and personality" may likewise be influenced by how neuronal development responds to experiences during infancy (Wiesel, 1982). In short, what we experience helps shape who we become.

As evolution proceeds and we deal with ever more complex organisms, experiences not only during early infancy but throughout an individual's entire life contribute increasingly to choices made. As the Nobel-Prize-winning neuroscientist Roger Sperry summarized the situation: "In regard to the inheritance of a given behaviour pattern, it is no longer so much a question of whether the machinery of growth is capable of installing it [in the brain], as to whether the survival rate [of the species] may be better if the behaviour is kept flexible by having it learned in each generation and thus adaptable to external conditions and adjustable to change" (Sperry, 1965).

Thus, we can see a definite trend in evolution from automatic, restricted ways of thinking toward expanding freedom of choice. But there is nothing inevitable about this. Such a trend will be continued if, and only if, humans choose wisely. If we imagine ourselves involved in our own evolution—which we are, whether conscious of it or not—it is in our own best interest to strive for two major aims: freedom and wisdom. Neither one nor the other alone is sufficient. Freedom without wisdom is destructive; wisdom without freedom—that is, the sealing forever of ancient wisdom against new insights—inhibits our ability to evolve further. Humans, more than any other organisms, have one singular gift: the capacity for vision. But even more wonderful is our ability to—in some instances—turn our visions into realities. The remainder of this essay will be concerned with the question of what these instances are, and how a transformation of vision into reality can be achieved.

The first and most important lesson a science-oriented approach to human progress teaches us is that cultural achievements are simply a continuation of biological evolution, not a disruption or even a contradiction of it.

Our dreams and inventions, the results of our brain activity, may lead us in the most diverse directions—some of them detrimental, regressive, or destructive, and others of magnificent, well-founded promise. Let us compare our minds' "creative sparks" during cultural evolution with mutations during biological evolution. The vast majority of random mutations are useless, and often they are lethal. Only if a mutation happens to fit into the exquisitely-balanced system of interactions of energy that are the hallmark of a living system will it survive and sometimes even be of advantage to the organism in which it occurs. Mutations are selected first and foremost for their capacity to work within a pre-existing system without disrupting or destroying it. One might even go so far as to say mutations are selected for their capacity to co-operate, to work in harmony with an organism's other pre-determined characteristics.

Creative sparks are similar. In a vacuum they die; in combination with unrealistic or irrational beliefs they may be lethal. Only when grounded in a solid understanding of reality—an understanding that must constantly be updated—do they allow humankind to progress. This is why we believe a constant checking and re-checking of vision and reality are necessary. History provides only too many examples. How lofty were the dreams of French and Russian revolutionaries, and how horrible was their bloodshed when human nature was not as they expected. Divorced from reality, creativity leads to self-destruction; grounded in a realistic understanding of human and non-human nature, it leads to the discovery of new worlds, both physically and mentally.

That our visions must fit into the existing reality system by no means indicates that they must fit into the reality system as we presently perceive it. Thorough-going readjustments to our perception of reality have had to be made in the past, often because of our species' gift for imagination and vision. Such changes of perception are initiated—or forced upon us—through the discovery of facts that are incompatible with our view of the world. For instance, in 450 B.C., the Greek historian Herodotus recorded reports of sailors who said that, as they ventured farther and farther down the coast of Africa, they eventually observed the high noon sun to their north, not to the south. "I do not believe it," Herodotus said cautiously of the tale, "but I write it down here nevertheless. Maybe someone else will believe it." Today, of course, we do believe the sailors' account, because our view of the world has changed since the time of Herodotus—from an image of a flat region surrounding the Mediterranean to one of a globe suspended in space.

Similarly, for decades the ancient Egyptians tried without success, using the most complicated calculations, to bring the newly invented calendar, which was based upon observations of the sky, into accord with the traditional calendar, based on the flooding of the Nile. It was all to no avail, until it occurred to some genius that, perhaps, the sun and the stars were more accurate timekeepers than the river's floods.

Such enlargements of man's worldview have taken place throughout history. Once the earth was the center of the universe, with the sun revolving around it. Before evolutionary theory was developed, biologists thought of species as fixed and unchanging. Before Einstein devised the theory of relativity, Newton's laws of motion reigned supreme. In each case, it was never nature that changed, only our perception of it; and in each case, the new and more realistic perception depended on a larger, more encompassing perspective. That wider perspective allowed us to account for facts previously thought inexplicable and to do things once thought impossible. There is no reason to assume that such advances will not continue, unless, of course, we advance in the wrong direction, toward the degradation or destruction of our species or the biosphere as a whole. And it cannot be denied that this is a real possibility.

Sixteen hundred scientists from leading academies in 70 countries, including 104 Nobel laureates—all persons of outstanding vision and creativity as well as realism—have reached a consensus that "human beings and the natural world are on a collision course." If we continue the present unrestricted growth in population and consumption, the earth will not be able to sustain our species much longer ("World Scientists' Warning to Humanity," 1993).

The disappearance of what was until then a vigorously-progressing species would not be unique in nature. It has happened before. Perhaps the best-known example occurred at the end of the Cretaceous, 70 million years ago, when the great reptiles we know as the dinosaurs, as well as many other plant and animal species, vanished from the geological record. But the dinosaurs were victims, felled (it is now thought) by the disruption brought on by the collision of an asteroid or comet with the earth. They didn't know what hit them, and even if, somehow, they had, they lacked the intelligence and wisdom to foresee dangers and prevent them. But we are different. Our problems are largely of our own making, and our brains developed enough to foresee dangers and devise solutions. To succeed in that task, however, we must rise above some prevailing presumptions and pre-conceptions.

For instance, if birth control is assumed to be a sin, as is still taught by one of the highest ethical authorities in the world (Ostling, 1993), there is no hope for our species. Even if we manage to produce more food, the starvation and social friction that accompany overcrowding will only be postponed—and there are additional problems which would remain unsolved. Roger Sperry has convincingly argued that population pressure in itself reduces the value of humankind:

> Rising demands for subsistence in a direly depleted, degraded ecosphere are not the sole concern. In numerous subtle and unsubtle ways overpopulation tends to desensitize humanity and demean the individual person as increasingly expendable. Our sense of the specialness of human life, its meaning, singular worth, dignity, and wonder undergoes an insidious, unobtrusive but inexorable erosion to which our inherent human nature is particularly vulnerable. The process is so slow and the habituation capacity of the human brain so great that the adverse trends, spread over decades or even generations, tend to be taken for granted. (Sperry, 1993)

Another of our preconceptions—that it is natural for humans to war against one another—is already being reconsidered. The danger of nuclear weapons is a powerful incentive to search for alternative solutions to disagreements.

One of the most serious dangers to our future, however, is the belief that constant economic growth is possible and desirable, and that it is the only way to achieve happiness. That belief, taken to heart by the billions of individuals already on the earth (even leaving aside the billions yet unborn) will, unless discovered to be erroneous, lead to a total collapse of the Earth's resources in a very short time.

It is on this problem that our ingenuity has to be focused, before survival and further evolution can even be discussed. (Population reduction is of similar importance, but here recent inventions, for instance that of Norplant, an implantable contraceptive device, are promising [Kantrowitz and Wingert, 1993]. The only difficulty remaining—albeit the most imposing one—is official disapproval.) We need an Einstein of economic theory—or rather of a new theory of human nature.

A study of human cultures shows that human beings need not necessarily be slaves of money-orientation. Not all such examples are palatable, to be sure. There are saints and Indian sages who derive happiness and ecstasy from martyrdom and sacrifices of their most basic needs. Such solutions are definitely undesirable as a standard for all human beings on earth. But there are also more constructive avenues for our minds and energies than either martyrdom or materialism. The psychologist Maslow conducted studies which demonstrated that, whenever one level of need was fulfilled, another, higher need came to the fore. At the base are physiological needs, such as sleep, hunger, sex, etc. Next is the need for safety, followed by the need for love and belongingness; higher yet is the need for esteem, and at the very apex is the need for "self-actualization." That last need is described by Maslow as impelling a person to perfect and use his or her special gifts. "A musician must make music, an artist must paint, a poet must write if he is ultimately to be at peace with himself" (Chaplin and Krawiec, 1968). —Here, we have a prescription for happiness that is independent of money, that is an end in itself, and that does not produce an insatiable thirst for more and more.

Maslow admits that persons achieving the highest level of fulfilment are rare, but all those who achieved it reported "peak experiences," states of extreme happiness and ecstasy, brought about simply by being able to enrich humanity with their gifts. According to Maslow, such outstanding human beings are not restricted to the world of artists; an athlete, a good workman, or a good mother, if they actualize their potentials to the fullest, may be lifted to the same heights of inner satisfaction. Further, he found that self-actualizers "demonstrate an efficient perception of reality and acceptance of it," that "they are creative" and that they are "autonomous and relatively independent of their environments." Thus, floods of advertisement or tempting displays of luxury would presumably not affect them.

We have here an image, a vision, of what it means to be "truly human or more than human," an ideal to strive for that has a realistic chance of succeeding: not maximum levels of wealth, but optimal amounts that provide for good health and education, and yet allow concern for our earth and our future. Not a life without problems, but a life that presents problems as challenges and their conquerors as heroes. Not a depleted, devastated earth filled to capacity with desperate people, but an optimal balance between the beauty and richness of our earth, and the vast and unexplored inner treasures of humankind.

While Maslow's "self-actualizers" are rare, it is nevertheless possible that the visions of a few motivate a large number of other persons. Charles Garfield, associate clinical professor at the University of California Medical School and head of a corporate consulting group, has described his experience as a team member involved in the building of the Apollo lunar excursion module in preparation for the first moon landing. "I started hearing stories about average people doing great work, performing way beyond anything they had done before. It turns out that there were over 30,000 people in multiple sites around the U.S. working on this project, averaging 30% to 40% increases in performance and productivity. The high achievers were making even bigger leaps. And what really perplexed me was that this was happening in a context in which we were poorly paid and the work conditions were lousy." This miraculous lift in spirits and capacities evaporated as soon as the project was completed. With Armstrong's first step on the moon, performance went down, motivation went down, and productivity went down among the working crew (Garfield, 1992).

We have here an example of a group of average, intelligent Americans, thoroughly indoctrinated with the prevalent idea that money is the major and only motivator and determinant of happiness, throwing all this overboard as soon as a really motivating and exciting project comes along. But they are not self-actualizers. As the motivating factor is withdrawn, moral collapses. —The same is true of many ethnic groups, whose zest for life vanishes with the destruction of their traditions and who are unable to find meaning in a lifestyle for which neither their nature nor their culture has prepared them. Rather than rejecting such thoughts as heretical, a thorough study of these facts would seem in order. A better understanding of this problem might lead to far more happiness, pride, and self-reliance among many present welfare recipients. (For instance a group of American Indians from Caughnawaga near Montreal has proved to be outstanding, and are much sought-for, as construction workers on New York skyscrapers, because of their absolute fearlessness of great heights.) Unbiased studies of human nature would also lead to a better understanding of how to improve our own life-experiences without destroying our earth. The prevalent talk of needed "sacrifices" is utterly self-defeating. Far greater success would be accomplished if the focus were shifted to the rewards inherent in a positive attitude toward the future: the joy of invention and creation, the renewed meaningfulness of existence.

We need a lasting goal toward which human dedication can be rallied, a vision with the power of paradise, and yet compatible with a scientist's understanding of the world. The greatest hope of finding such a goal lies in learning more about how we think.

As we have seen, the evolution of the brain proceeded along a trajectory from restricted, automatic decision-making among simpler animals like our friend the frog, to informed, involved choosing of various alternatives by higher primates like ourselves. With the acquisition of consciousness and culture, we have learned that the responsibility to continue that trend is now our own. That is not easy. Informed choices that demolish long-held preconceptions are violently rejected, even if they remove barriers to the progress of civilization.

David C. Korten (1992) describes the upheaval that occurred five hundred years ago, when Copernicus in the year of his death dared publish his theory that the earth is not the centre of the universe with the sun and the stars revolving around it, but simply one of the planets revolving around the sun, which itself is only one of countless stars in the sky. Humanity's central position in the universe was challenged, and Copernicus' point of view was vilified. But "his act and the resulting change in perspective regarding man's place in the cosmos, deflating as it was to a longstanding human arrogance, liberated Western society from a number of debilitating intellectual and institutional constraints, ushered in the age of science, and led to human accomplishments that have exceeded even the most fanciful imaginings of the greatest thinkers of his day." Korten suggests that present-day ecological problems may force us into another revolution of human thought that is sure to lead to new traumas and rejections, but "that will also release a new era of progress as far beyond the current human imagination as the accomplishment of the modern era would be to those who lived in the Middle Ages."

The new revolution of perception we need will not necessarily require a more encompassing look at the universe. It will require a deeper, more informed understanding of human nature.

Visions are vital. They liberate unknown potentials in the human brain. But unless we readjust our goals and targets from chasing mirages to pursuing realistic aims, our dreams will delude us and leave us poorer and more desperate than before. We cannot fill the earth with more people than it can decently support. We cannot aim for unlimited material growth. Between these two constraints of reality lies a vast and unexplored region of creativity and mental advance. To safeguard and further that advance and creativity must become our highest and most sacred goal.

REFERENCES

Chaplin, J.P., and Krawiec, T.S., 1968. *Systems and Theories of Psychology* (Maslow's hierarchical theory of motivation, pp. 428-432). New York: Holt, Rinehart and Winston.

Csikszentmihalyi, M., 1991. "Consciousness for the 21st Century." *Zygon*, 26, 1-26.

Garfield, C. 1992. "Second to None: Business in the Ecological Age." *Noetic Sciences Review*, No. 24 (Winter), 15-19.

Hubel, D.H. and Wiesel, T.N. 1962. "Receptive Fields, Binocular Interaction and Functional Architecture in the Cat's Visual Center." *Journal of Physiology*, 160: 106-154.

Kantrowitz, B. and Wingert, P. 1993. "The Norplant Debate." *Newsweek*, February 15, 1993, 37-41.

Korten, D.C. 1992. "Development, Heresy, and the Ecological Revolution." *Context*, No. 33 (Summer 1992), 50.

Ostling, R.N. 1993. "A Refinement of Evil." Time, October 4, 1993, 54.

Sperry, R.W. 1965. "Embryogenesis of Behavioral Nerve Nets." In R.L. Deehan and H. Ursprung, eds., *Organogenesis*. Holt, Rinehart and Winston, New York, pp. 161-85.

Sperry, R.W. 1993. "The Impact and Promise of the Cognitive Revolution." *American Psychologist* (August 1993), 878-885.

Thoreau, H.D. *Walden*. 1906. In *The Writings of Henry David Thoreau*. Boston: Houghton Mifflin.

Wiesel, T.N. 1982. "Postnatal Development of the Visual Cortex and the Influence of the Environment." [Nobel Lecture.] *Nature*, 299: 583-591.

"World Scientists' Warning to Humanity" (1993). Available through Union of Concerned Scientists, 26 Church Street, Cambridge, MA 02238.

CHAPTER ELEVEN

The Co-evolutionary Research Ideology

One of Erdmann's favourite stories from the history of science involved the longstanding dispute over the causes of infectious disease. Was it bacteria that made people sick, or were lack of cleanliness and hygiene, particularly in those sections of Victorian cities that were home to the working classes, the root causes of disease? In the end, both factors were proven to play a role. In this essay, written for the December 2001 issue of The Path, *a newsletter published by Kathia and Alexander Laszlo's Syntony Quest organization, Erika drew a broader lesson for today's world from the search for the root causes of disease. (Syntony Quest was founded with the aim of fostering new approaches to work and life grounded in an understanding of evolutionary theory, and Alexander Laszlo and Erika corresponded regularly during the last years of her life.) As the Laszlos noted in their introductory blurb, the co-evolutionary research ideology "challenges us to think in terms of 'both-and' rather than 'either-or,' invites us to engage in participative forms of enquiry, and reminds us to keep an open mind and a future orientation. [Erdmann's] views are refreshing and empowering and we thought they would be a wonderful holiday gift."*

One statement stands out in my mind, a statement I found in "Learning to Become" by Alexander and Kathia Laszlo (*Creating Learning Communities*, Ron Miller, ed., 2000): "Evolutionary Learning Communities do not adapt their environments to their needs nor do they simply adapt to their environments. Rather, they adapt with their environment in a dynamic of mutually sustaining evolutionary co-creation."

How much in tune with my life's preoccupation!

Contrasting basic assumptions lie at the root of many unresolvable conflicts. Do we have a tool, a science, or anything of that kind which deals with the correction of erroneous basic assumptions? I believe that the "co-evolutionary research ideology," as described by the philosopher of science Patricia Churchland (1986), comes closest to what we need to overcome both a blind forward rush into unforeseen dangers and resignation to unfortunate developments we can foresee.

The co-evolutionary research ideology, which has greatly contributed to success in science, encourages the approach of two opposing theories towards a common position closer to the truth than either one alone. It works through a method in which successful research results in pursuit of one of these theories elicit new insights, adjustments, and research designs in the opposing theory. These new findings, in turn, illuminate and adjust the former, and so on, until the best possible approach to the truth is reached. Often, neither of the original theories has to be abolished, but each is enriched and enlightened by the opposing one.

An example is the theory that poverty and slums cause diseases vs. the theory that diseases are caused by germs—two views which in the last half of the 19th century were fighting each other fanatically. We now know that poverty and slums cause diseases because germs proliferate under these conditions. There is no reason left why one of these theories should be defended against the other one. If such methods could be applied to solve political and ideological disagreements, wars will become unnecessary and humanity will have made an immense step forward.

The drama of the "slum vs. germ" controversy, which I traced with the help of several encyclopedias at the library of the California Institute of Technology, is unforgettable. I am using here the original compilation from my encyclopedia notes:

> An excellent example is the fight, raging during the second half of the 19th century, between the pioneer of bacteriology, Nobel laureate Robert Koch, and the medical authority Rudolf Virchow. At its height, the battle involved almost every medical institute on all continents. The two sides approached the problem from much different perspectives. Koch and his disciples remained glued to the microscope and discovered bacterial causes of disease after disease. Virchow, on the other hand, was convinced that diseases are caused by poverty and neglect. He had cleaned up the slums of Berlin and transformed the city from one of the dirtiest in the world to one of the cleanest in only two decades. Pointing to the drastic reduction in illness his measures had produced, he rejected Koch's evidence. So deeply ingrained was his conviction that either bacteria alone or poverty alone caused disease that he—the man considered the world's leader in his field, the man for whom an entire institute had been built in the city of Berlin—forbade the study of bacteriology in his institute. He approached the problem from a different level, one in which bacteria had no place. So adamant was his conviction that he still refused to change his mind even when bacteriology became an accepted course in all major medical institutes. Finally, confronted with the choice of either permitting courses in bacteriology or resigning, Virchow resigned.
>
> At some point someone asked the question: Under which conditions do bacteria thrive best? That question led to a step-by-step approach toward a superior middle position: poverty and neglect cause diseases because bacteria proliferate in unsanitary slum conditions, and because poverty and neglect lower resistance against them. Today, it is hard to understand how such a self-evident solution could have been missed at the outset, and how the contrast of viewpoints could have led to such violent fights.

Another controversy raged during the middle of the next century, and around another famous man of science, E. O. Wilson. Wilson had been fascinated by snakes and insects since childhood, had studied their behavior thoroughly, and had written a large and meticulously researched tome on the subject, called *Sociobiology*. It had barely been published when attacks on it flared up all over the world. Wilson had extrapolated from insects directly to humans and had implied that, because deceit occurred in lower animals, it was a natural survival device of evolution and can therefore not be rejected as evil in humans. Goodness is based on self-deceit. —But in contrast to Virchow, Wilson learned from his opponents—especially from one very kind, intelligent, and understanding person, R. W. Burhoe (a good friend of mine with whom I had many conversations on the subject). Burhoe convinced his opponent—and later his friend—that in humans, culture, an evolutionary device absent in animals, has become a major influence on behavior, in the absence of which we could not exist. So thorough was Wilson's conversion, that his latest book, *Consilience*, does not even mention *Sociobiology* (on which he had worked half of his life) in his autobiographical blurb. I have read both books and am astonished by their different outlook and about Wilson's humility. He describes the intoxication of a scientific discovery, the shell it builds around the discoverer's mind, and the difficulty of penetrating that shell with new evidence—all from personal experience. Yet he succeeded in breaking it. Consilience goes beyond the co-evolutionary research ideology, which is concerned only with science. Wilson writes: "Most of the issues that vex humanity daily—ethnic conflict, arms escalation, overpopulation, abortion, environment, endemic poverty, to cite several most persistently before us—cannot be solved without integrating knowledge from the natural sciences with that of the social sciences and the humanities. Only fluency across the boundaries will provide a clear view of the world as it really is, not seen through the lens of ideologies and religious dogmas or commanded by myopic response to immediate need."

What is the difference between Virchow and Wilson? —An open mind!

An open mind is the foundation for humanity's survival and development.

Again, we are confronted with a controversy, far more dangerous than the ones described above, even more dangerous than any that existed before. It is a dichotomy of political convictions in an age of nuclear, chemical, and biological weapons. On the one side, fanatical terrorists sacrifice their lives in a frenzy of terrible destruction; on the other, righteous and revenge-hungry statesmen divide the entire world into two parts: "Either you are for us, or you are for the terrorists." There is nothing in between.

Is it possible to arrive at a middle position between these two extremes, superior to both of them? I see a faint hope at the horizon. It has been called "capitalism with a conscience" by one of my friends and subscribers to *Humankind Advancing*, Raymond Schiller, and it is a point of view in which freedom co-exists with interior convictions of right and wrong that would prevent excesses. For instance, the skillful targeting of young, unformed minds to instill desire for unneeded things, built-in obsolescence, and many more devices to make money at the expense of our environment and our future would be perceived as revolting, just as we are now revolted by the thought that stealing and murder ought to be permitted in the name of freedom. In fact, such interior restrictions on freedom are the only guarantors for its lasting existence. Nor does "capitalism with a conscience" allow concentration on money-making to overrule concern for our fellow-beings. In such a system, the accumulation of money is never merely an aim in itself. Money has value only as a means to achieve a worthwhile and fulfilling life.

The most beautiful, worthwhile, and fulfilling life, I believe, is one that rises above preoccupation with short-term personal success to concern with the success of our species. Here, constant adjustment of dream and reality is necessary, and constant learning about the nature of reality. During biological evolution, the effect of emerged phenomena upon each other resulted in eye sight. Let us hope and work for a new emergent form of cultural evolution: *mind sight*—the ability to foresee and avoid dangers, especially the extinction of our species, and the ability to discern and encourage new and promising initiatives. That is what Syntony Quest is all about, and why it is so urgently needed.

CHAPTER TWELVE

In Search of Values for Human Survival

If in her master's thesis (later revised and published as Beyond a World Divided) *Erdmann examined the gap between science and human values, with a special focus on how Roger Sperry's work on consciousness might bridge that gap, then in her doctoral dissertation she widened her perspective to consider suggestions from other thinkers on this same topic. As noted in Chapter One, the dissertation made use of the ideas of thinkers such as Sperry and Ralph Burhoe as a jumping-off point for a deeper exploration of the values animating North American society in general and, in particular, that society's response to global problems such as overpopulation, resource depletion, and economic inequality. She singled out as particularly important the finding that even when people shared the same underlying values, they might espouse vastly different actions in response to a given situation. "Therefore [she wrote] not values themselves,* but the perception of reality from which they arise and through which they are interpreted and translated into action *[emphasis the editor's], must demand our main attention." This, it seems to me, is a crucial insight, and one which has much to say about our ongoing difficulties in tackling global problems that have only become more acute in the quarter-century since Erika wrote those words.*

A briefer version of the dissertation was published in 1989 in Peace Research Reviews, *and a summary article, "Values Needed for Survival," in the book* Hopes and Fears: The Human Future *(Samuel Stevens, 1992). The excerpts here first set out the parameters of her research project, then go on to sum up its findings and insights.*

Institutions responsible for the creation and maintenance of human values and belief systems, such as schools, universities, churches, and the mass media, are with few exceptions still going about the task completely oblivious of the most important question that present developments have forced us to ask: "What are the values we need for the survival of mankind?"

In 1981, 36 years after the first atomic bomb had been dropped on Hiroshima, nine years after the first Club of Rome report on the need to restrict unlimited growth had been published, I discovered that not a single professor of the department of philosophy at one of the largest and most prestigious universities of the North American continent had addressed himself to that question in his curriculum or could even tell me who had.

If this attitude is indicative of universities or other value-shaping institutions in general—and part of my project will be a start to investigating that matter—it is no wonder that answers to this most important question are met with indifference and misunderstanding. Our first task must therefore be to effect a turnover of human thought—practically a plowing of the mental field—to make it receptive for the impact of mankind's best, most concerned, and most responsible members.

The second task must be to encourage a natural integration of relevant work in progress so that those concerned with theoretical fundaments are not left without means of implementation and those with ideas of practical implementation are not stranded without any fundaments upon which to ground them.

It is hoped that the present study will help to turn the search for workable, survival-oriented values into the most fascinating, challenging pursuit of a progress-oriented society—that it will help to initiate further work which may lead to a re-evaluation of the entire concept of advance.

STATEMENT OF PRECONCEPTIONS

From the beginning of my work on the present project I decided to approach all answers without preconceptions or plans in order to open my mind fully to the learning experience I would derive from them. What I learned was considerable. Among other lessons, I was instructed that no objective approach to a research project is possible, that lifetime experiences cannot be erased even from consciousness—not to speak of the subconscious—and that therefore the most honest approach to any project should begin with a statement of the researcher's preconceptions, so that these can be taken into account while reading his or her work (Jones, 1980).

My own preconceptions are the following: Progress in evolution proceeds through blind trial and error. Innumerable dead ends are witness to erratic attempts that ended in failure. Ninety-nine percent of all species that ever evolved are no more. Nature, having arrived at a point of decision about humankind, asks for our cooperation. *For the first time in the history of evolution, blind trial and error can be augmented by conscious choice.* "What are the values needed to guide human action?" If we answer wisely, our chances to survive and to further evolve are good. If we answer foolishly or not at all, the overwhelming chances are that we will be channelled into a dead end.

J. Piatt (1983, p. 28) compares our progress through evolution at the present time with a canoe trip through the foaming, boiling waters of a canyon. Rocks and boulders, partly visible and partly submerged, produce dangerous whirlpools and call for the utmost skill and vigilance of the pilot. —I see the rocks as dogmas, the whirlpools as illusions, and mankind in desperate need of capable pilots.

Dogmas are the ultimate wisdom of a certain time period which may become dangerous in a different time. We need a philosophy that goes beyond dogmas. The one I consider most fruitful has been worked out by Roger Sperry, whose view of reality goes beyond the awesome but empty and purposeless universe presented through traditional science to include ideas and ideals as products of the interplay of natural forces in the brain. Like all other events in nature, these ideas and ideals have a force, power, and causality of their own; they are creative and active. —Empathy commands our hands to help, wisdom our brains to consider the consequences of our choices. —That is his science, not cold and meaningless, but elevated by thought and sentiments emergent from insentient nature.

> In the eyes of science, to put it simply, man's creator becomes the vast interwoven fabric of all evolving nature, a tremendously complex concept that includes all the immutable and emergent forces of cosmic causation that control everything from high-energy sub-nuclear particles to galaxies, not forgetting the causal properties that govern brain function and behavior at individual, interpersonal, and social levels. For all these, science has gradually become our accepted authority, offering a cosmic scheme and view of the human psyche that renders most others simplistic by comparison and which grows and evolves as science advances. (Sperry, 1985, p. 114)

". . . That grows and evolves as science advances." There is no room for rigid beliefs that turn into dangerous obstacles.

Illusions are created by ideals disregarding reality. Boulding (1978) warns:

> With what might be called the radical passion one must have sympathy. The passion to eliminate poverty, misery, hunger, malnutrition, and avoidable ill health, and to create a world in which every person born has a reasonable opportunity to fulfil the genetic potential for health and learning, love and joy, grief and resignation, is a passion in tune with the potential of the human race. But we have to admit, however unwillingly and unpleasantly, that passion is frequently, but not necessarily, the enemy of truth, and that passion distorts our image of the world often to the point where our illusions prevent fulfilment of the passion. It is the radical illusions, not the conservative coldness, that are the greatest enemies of the radical passion. If the radical passion is to be fulfilled, if we are indeed to move into a world that is better than what we have now, the radical illusions must be discarded and a realistic appraisal of the dynamic effects of human actions must become widespread. (p. 356)

The need for pilots is most succinctly described by Jonas Salk (1963): "In the face of the magnitude of our problems, we are in deep need of recognizing extraordinary human beings."

As a first step in the dangerous voyage ahead I have discarded my own illusion that objective research is possible and stated my preconceptions frankly and openly. As a second step [in the original text of the dissertation] I will list the responses I received for each category separately . . . before I discuss them, so that anyone may have access to them and see new rocks and whirlpools, or new potential pilots, in the light of his or her different experiences and preconceptions before their outlines become clouded through my own interpretations. . . .

The voyage will lead into the minds of some of the most influential persons on a continent which has at present the greatest impact on global matters.

At the end of the dissertation, Erdmann summarized the research project's key findings and drew out the insights it suggested:

The following three questions were asked to provoke thought about the values guiding our actions and to receive answers that might lead us into a more promising direction.

1. What are the values needed for the survival of mankind?
2. What are the possibilities and limitations of human nature?
3. What is the best way to implement needed new values?

Ten sectors of North American society were addressed: religion, philosophy, science, the humanities, the mass media, persons promoting science-religion interaction, peace activists, researchers, and advocates, persons advocating a sustainable society, persons advocating technological progress, and "other concerned persons." The first five sectors were selected because they determine and consolidate existing values, the next five because they are future-oriented. As far as possible, persons in leading positions were approached, each through a personal letter, a printed questionnaire containing the above three questions with explanations, and—to receive some feedback from those whose time would not permit them to supply personal statements—a photocopied answer sheet, containing six answers to be checked.

The first pair of answers gave reasons either for or against the usefulness of the project, the second pair favored either traditional religion or traditional science, the third pair was in favour of (a) a combination of values *and* objective knowledge, and (b) elevated the former through a larger perspective, involving our biosphere and future generations. In the formulation of the answers, predominance was given to the provoking of thought over statistical simplicity. The aim was not to count opinions, but to elicit, and receive, original contributions.

Seven hundred and sixteen letters reached their intended recipient, and 221 responses were received, the majority of which consisted of comments, letters, articles, or books (sent or recommended) instead of, or in addition to, filled-out questionnaires. (The overall response rate was 30.9%.) . . . Responses from the peace sector were most numerous (61.1%), slowly declining over science-religion interaction, religion, other concerned persons, sustainable society, philosophy, technological progress, science, humanities, and the mass media (the latter with a response rate of 15.4%). To have a basis for adequate comparison of viewpoints but be nevertheless able to handle the voluminous feedback, letters to any one sector were discontinued after the first 20 answers were received.

The main body of the project consists of the quotes selected from comments, letters, books, or papers, and their discussion. The selection criterion for quotes was their relevance to our species' survival and its quality. Summarizing all responses, I decided to be led by the suggestion of G. D. Kaufman (respondent #1 in the religion sector), that we must "work together toward the common goal and the common good, drawing upon whatever resources—religious or secular, philosophical or poetic, mythic or scientific—are available to us, and offering them to each other as we grope toward an unknown future."

What, then, are the resources *Religion* has to offer?

Expressed in two short words, the greatest contribution from the sector of religion can be described as INSIGHT and COURAGE. Insight is provided through silent concentration in prayer, courage through the filtering of wisdom from new knowledge and its admittance to the magnificent body of old wisdom. That courage is expressed predominantly by Kaufman in his book *Theology for a Nuclear Age*, where he maintains that God and humanity will either live or perish together. —Other responses show reliance upon faith in providence; it is believed that we are in the care of a supernatural God.

The need for LOVE and COMPASSION, the traditional gifts of religion to humanity, find ample expression in this sector too, but, fortunately, they are not restricted to it. Not a single one of the ten categories questioned was without the answer that love and compassion are needed for human survival—usually repeated by several different respondents. To survive, however, humanity has to learn to combine love and compassion with knowledge to achieve wisdom.

What, therefore, are the resources of *Philosophy*, the ancient wellspring of wisdom?

The need for FREEDOM, INTELLIGENCE, REASON, common sense, and common HUMAN DECENCY were expressed or implied, but a surprisingly large number of philosophers responded that they could neither understand nor answer my questions. Yes, wisdom and the need for EDUCATION were mentioned too, as in nearly all other sectors, including religion. For drawing attention to the danger of dogmatism and to the danger of introducing new dogmas (considerations which strongly influenced my work on the project), I am grateful to respondent #4, whose answer emphasized the need for tolerance.

Reference to the need to check unlimited population increase and the need to check unlimited acquisition of material wealth is made for the first time in the sector of philosophy, although warnings regarding the second need are one of religion's most ancient tasks; it is implicit in much of the work received, especially in Nouwen's papers. Again, respondents from all sectors are vividly aware of these two major problems.

Outstanding among the answers of philosophers is the expression of the need for RESPONSIBILITY, a value also repeatedly demanded through other sectors. Responsibility for our human future, however, as requested by Jonas, Hook, the Dalai Lama, and others leads to differing and contrasting recommendations for action depending upon the responsible agent's perception of reality.

Most remarkable is Ervin Laszlo's insight into the need for PRAGMATIC GROUND RULES, which should include policies bringing about POSITIVE-SUM RESULTS among other basic goods (sustainability, development, equity). Anything less, he maintains, would not stem the trend toward increasingly desperate conditions; anything more would constitute attempts at social engineering and do more harm than good. Laszlo's main concern is with the disadvantaged part of humanity, but his suggestions provide a large step forward from Communist dictatorships. Should the "co-evolutionary research ideology" be at work here? (See the comment in the "Insights" section below, second paragraph, and also Churchland, 1936, p. 363.)

If so, the complementary step from the opposing side should be encouraged by drawing special attention to Kupperman's verdict that "intelligence is the most dangerous product of evolution". . . . What is dangerous is intelligence in isolation, intelligence that excludes common sense approaches, love and compassion. Inclusive intelligence turns into wisdom and becomes the most promising value of humanity. Wisdom would encourage the mutual approach of basic assumptions at present still fundamentally incompatible.

Laszlo already attempts the admirable but nearly impossible task of finding common denominators among widely contrasting world views with the aim to achieve global solidarity. To draw adequate attention to the importance and the immense difficulty of his undertaking, an disproportionate amount of space has been devoted here to his work. It is urgently recommended to study thoroughly both the original "Global Goals and Values Reports" and Laszlo's conclusions from them in his "Goals for Mankind." The study of either alone is insufficient and leads to contrasting results: that of the former to the opinion that the task is impossible, that of the latter to the belief that it is easy and can be taken for granted. It is, however, immensely difficult, if it can be achieved at all at the present stage of human thinking habits. If to wait seems too dangerous or even counterproductive, an alternative might be the provision of a new world view or perception of reality which is so convincing and provides so much hope for our future that older visions fade away like the stars in the night sky during the rise of the sun.

Can *Science* provide such a view? What are its resources?

One of its most basic contributions can probably be described as the CO-EVOLUTIONARY RESEARCH IDEOLOGY, the approach toward the truth from contrasting assumptions through objective research which underlies all scientific progress, and which would provide the best hope for progress in human thinking habits in general.

Directly recommended were obligations toward society, hope for our future through GREATER UNDERSTANDING OF THE HUMAN MIND, and OPTIMISM regarding human nature, especially its CAPACITY FOR CRITICAL THINKING, among other qualities. Moreover, hope for evolution toward greater humanity is expressed. Such evolution may not be biological, but cultural and dependent upon the extension of objective knowledge.

"With each new phase of synthesis to emerge from biological inquiry," E. O. Wilson says, "the humanities will expand their reach and capability."

The major contribution of science, however, is its call for OPENMINDEDNESS, for the acceptance and critical assessment of all new ideas, whether or not they coincide with one's system of belief. The great asset of science is its concept of progression in nature, the idea of evolution, the rejection of a static world, of absolutes, of dogmas. Although science was, and probably still is, riddled by errors, the process of error elimination as the most promising way into the future (impressively described by Salk [1983] in his *Anatomy of Reality*) provides a beacon of hope among the promotion of rigid adherence to systems that cannot and must not be changed, even if humanity is to perish as a result. The great disadvantage of science is that it concentrates—and *must* concentrate to ensure the continuation of its phenomenal success—on things that can be measured and counted. It therefore leaves out phenomena of major impact upon mankind, such as subjective experience.

As a consequence, the great equalizer of human perception across different local ideological fanaticisms is also recognized and feared as the great degrader which erases from humanity the most beautiful and most sacred aspects of its existence. Perhaps, it is no coincidence that the first DANGER SIGNAL, the first expression of the conviction that man does not deserve to survive, comes from the sector of science. A vacuum is experienced where traditional ideologies found the essence of mankind they called the soul.

To fill that vacuum, we have to direct our attention to resources from the *Humanities.*

E. Mann-Borgese suggests designating the oceans as "common heritage of mankind" and keeping them free from private ownership—a first step toward the introduction of that concept worldwide, which she conceives as advancement toward justice. —Garrett Hardin would disagree. For him, the "tragedy of the commons" lies in the exploitation of conscientious persons by irresponsible egoists, in the disappearance of the former, and the increase of the latter. —Proper management and laws might avoid that tragedy; moreover, private ownership is no safeguard against injustice. Values *and* laws are needed to achieve fair and decent living conditions. To both, Mann-Borgese gives much thought.

In addition to love and respect for human beings, TOLERANCE is requested by the present sector, and attention is drawn to the ubiquitous Will to Power, which lies at the root of all our most intractable problems.

On the whole, however, it is tempting to respond to the answers received from the persons of the humanities sector with another big question: Where are the poets, the dramatists, the great writers of the present who move and shake our emotions, who determine our decisions? Where are those who compensate for the emptiness of science instead of being led by it? (Of course, I do not expect that my small survey would have touched such persons, but they could at least have been recommended.) One respondent (from the sector "other concerned persons") intuitively felt that void when he recommended Plato, Shakespeare, and Goethe. Yet these great masters lived in a time of comparative global peace and safety. Should not their counterparts speak out as the world is being torn apart? —Or are their voices unheard because the mass media consider them too exclusive to sell well enough? —How would Plato, Shakespeare, or Goethe have fared had they had to depend on mass appeal instead of selective evaluation by outstanding persons?

We have to turn next, therefore, to views and resources from the *Mass Media*.

The attitudes of the few who responded positively were not notably different from those of other sectors. In addition to values previously mentioned, attention was drawn for the first time to the need for KNOWLEDGE, TRUTH, and UNDERSTANDING. —But how representative are these voices of the major attitudes motivating the mass media?

Although they could be one of the most promising tools of world unification, the predominant attitude of the mass media seems to be one of rejection of responsibility. Money orientation as guideline and determinant of action is taken for granted. The alternative, it is maintained, would be an authoritarian government with all its disadvantages directing the media.

There must be a third way out, and to search for it is one of the most urgent tasks. Extraordinary persons exist, and our future depends on the impact of their thoughts. Perhaps private groups, such as the "Better World Society," a new and hopeful development combining global consciousness with television programming, could gain sufficient influence to counterbalance the pervasive money orientation which threatens to drain humanity of most of its value.

Among those who clearly see the danger of a world without meaning, a world toward which we move through the domination of science and the money orientation of the mass media, are promoters of *Science-Religion-Interaction*. What are the resources they have to offer?

This small but highly motivated group of men and women is convinced that science alone, and appeal to rationality alone, are insufficient to guide human action. As D. Campbell puts it: "Awe-inspiring indoctrination is needed to produce morally committed persons." Traditional religion, however, has lost its ability to counterbalance short-sighted wishes and desires because its credibility is maimed through its adherence to ancient and superseded explanations of nature. Modern minds, who reject these explanations, reject with them religion itself. To regain the power of religion, it is necessary to update it and to bring it into accord with the world view of science. God, therefore, is equated with nature's creative forces active in the evolving universe, which include those within the human brain and mind.

RESPONSIBILITY, again, becomes one of the highest values, next to the study and knowledge of the laws of nature to which humankind has to be obedient to succeed as a species. The habit of TRUTH is exalted. In the words of B. Davis, "Distortion of the facts does not pay, for nature always has the last word." To condense the contribution of this group into one short phrase, it may be expressed as THE REVIVAL OF HIGHER GUIDANCE FOR HUMAN ACTION.

The advantage of this point of view is that no rejection of God is possible. Dissent from the laws of nature is met with immediate punishment, independent of belief or disbelief in their power. —There is one difficulty, however. The discourse among the group's members usually exists at an academic level quite inaccessible to the general public. Although there are exceptions, such as the moving passage by M. R. Lemberg speaking of selfless service to humanity without the expectation to be remembered for it, and although the need to revive such values as love and compassion underlies and carries the entire mission of the group, missing is the simple, clear and concise language that would carry the group's message across the world, a world in urgent need of the wisdom upon which peace can be built.

The longing for *Peace* and the vivid visualization of the probable dangers of a war in the nuclear age is most strongly expressed through the members of various peace groups united in the that sector, the sector most responsive to the question for survival-oriented values. What are its gifts?

We receive from the Assistant to the Secretary General of the United Nations, Robert Mueller, OPTIMISM, the precious attitude able to discern the advantages of even the most gloomy situation; we receive from Hanna and Alan Newcombe REALISM, an essential quality that rejects both despair and excessive, superficial confidence—and we receive WISDOM, the highest value needed for the survival of mankind. Not only is that value recognized and beautifully expressed, but also lived by the Newcombes and many other workers for peace. While most respondents suggested "education" as the best way to implement needed new values, Alan Newcombe asks that we "let our lives stand as witnesses." Moreover, it is he who enriches our list of values needed for human survival with empathy, trust, and TRUSTWORTHINESS.

Furthermore, the need for intelligence is repeated again; T. E. Jones notes that "one correct opinion is worth more than many incorrect ones" and that "incompatible assumptions" lead to conflicting forecasts and recommendations for the future. Wherever it can be obtained, empirical evidence is proscribed as an antidote.

The major contribution of the peace sector, however, is the quest for a GLOBAL CONSCIOUSNESS and CONCERN FOR FUTURE GENERATIONS.

There are nevertheless several DANGER SIGNALS emitted from this sector. Steps to be taken are suggested without adequate consideration of values and qualities that might be lost from mankind forever as a consequence. It is believed that revolution may succeed where reason fails, and that civil disobedience can work against an utterly ruthless opponent. Furthermore (not suggested in this section but by a peace worker under "other concerned persons") it is believed that unilateral disarmament may secure peace on earth or that it at least would guarantee the survival of future generations. —All that is questionable. Unless workable values for human survival can be found and accepted, revolutions will turn the oppressed into oppressors, civil disobedience will systematically eliminate persons from our earth who obey their conscience, and unilateral disarmament will free the way only for vicious fights among dissenting factions of the victorious side—with or without nuclear, biological, or chemical tools of war. The danger to mankind will be no less than before.

In further search for the values we need, we will now turn to the sector that perhaps incorporates the greatest hope for humankind: promoters of a *Sustainable Society*.

Their outstanding attitude is CONCERN FOR FUTURE GENERATIONS and CONCERN FOR OUR ENTIRE BIOSPHERE. Most are realists. While scientists and economists tend to see unrestricted population increase as the source of all our problems, and while waste of resources, greed, and excessive wealth is selectively condemned from the side of religion and socialism, promoters of a sustainable society have, in general, arrived at the insight that both of these phenomena will lead to disaster. Moreover, success in the elimination of one of these problems is impossible unless the other one is also in retreat. Voluntary population reduction cannot rationally be expected, or even promoted, while resources are squandered. Likewise, no appeal to help for the hungry will be very effective if the result turns out to be more rapid population increase and more hungry people on earth.

Three quests are new: The demand for more FEMALE PARTICIPATION in all decision-making (scientific, corporate, and governmental); the demand for MODERN-DAY PROPHETS who combine the wisdom of the ancients with new knowledge; and the demand to discuss values, not in isolation, but in their relation to perceptions of reality. Ophuls doubts that democracy is able to rise above narrow, and destructive, self-interest, while Barker recommends it as the only means to consider special circumstances while applying general maxims. That general maxims, or values, are needed, however, is emphatically endorsed by everyone.

Nevertheless, a moderate DANGER SIGNAL also looms at the horizon. A few persons in love with the biosphere . . . tend to see the human being as a parasite, whose elimination from the earth would be a blessing. These persons forget that the experience of beauty, of love, and of compassion is a creation of the human nervous system and would be eliminated from our earth—and maybe from the universe—with the elimination of humankind. —Our task is not to eliminate, but to strengthen these assets of humanity.

The main contribution of promoters of a sustainable society consists in the rational insight that the earth is too small for the free range of all innate or conditioned whims, wishes, and desires of human beings, and that values and laws to curb them are necessary to avoid severe degradation of humankind.

Another sector of persons concerned with our future, those in favor of *Technological Progress*, disagrees: Our task must be, not to curb, but to expand human desires and imaginations; not to mistrust, but to TRUST HUMAN INGENUITY; not to withdraw ourselves into the envelope of our earth's capacity, but to expand into the universe. Emphasis is placed on humankind's ability to think, to invent, to innovate. Boundless OPTIMISM seems to predominate. Much can be done, even here on earth. The invention of synthetic food is only one example. Bacard advocates hunger for power, but interprets it as hunger to make significant contributions to mankind. Reason and intelligence, of course, are promoted, but also COOPERATION (Axelrod). Hayek, on the other hand, exalts competition—seemingly oblivious of the fact that the same competition which has led our civilization to cultural heights may with the discovery of the finiteness of our resources reward only irresponsibility.

There are examples of the very emptiness and meaninglessness of science which is most feared—but also of profound concern with human beings here on earth. —The hallmark of the sector, however, is its thirst for expansion into outer space.

An inexhaustible wellspring of ideas (the expression is Piatt's) seems to be active.

Whether even one one-thousandth of then would work is questionable; nevertheless, every advance in civilization has its source in ideas originally rejected as Utopian—as Drexler dramatically documents in his *Engines of Creation.* Responsible persons, such as Picht, warn that the costs of the projects suggested would be prohibitive. No doubt, ideas are and will be in ample supply; but the costs of implementing then would demand unacceptable sacrifices of mankind. Would it be rational to let most of humanity die of starvation to afford space colonization for a tiny percentage of them? —Moreover, we have not now any enemies from outer space—should we try to provide them? Would it not be most rational for persons cramped into space stations to return to our lovely earth after decades of disappointments on other planets and treat us as we treated the inhabitants of discovered continents?

On the other hand, space colonization is perceived as the ultimate expression of human freedom, as the ultimate solution of our overpopulation problem, as the ultimate victory of the human spirit over oppressing bondages, as the ultimate security system for our species. Once the sun expands into a red giant in another five billion years, once it envelops the earth and other planets in its devastating heat, human beings will not have to cease to exist. They will have found other planets on which to survive and further evolve; they will have acquired the capability to build their own planets in accord with the requirements of their nature. There will be no wars; human reason will have evolved far enough to avoid them. The vastness of the universe will make wars superfluous.

Which of these two attitudes should be promoted? The decision is difficult. It seems not only impossible, but also criminal, to bring about the cessation of human flights of imagination—and yet they may carry the seeds of the destruction of mankind. Let us hope and pray that we will find means to discover and protect what is best for humanity.

Should that hope remain unfulfilled, all other hopes will vanish, all other questions be asked in vain. Long before the first space colony can be tested, hatred and irrationality will have eradicated all of mankind, together with its soaring thoughts. The greatest demand, therefore, is for voices of wisdom; the greatest mistake to silence these voices in favour of the acquisition of material wealth.

Having heard the recommendations of nine different sectors of our society, let us now turn to *Other Concerned Persons*, human beings selected not because of their common background, but because of their common aim: concern for the future of mankind.

One answer stands out: Not values in isolation, but PERCEPTIONS OF REALITY guiding them determine recommendations for action. All respondents from this sector have nearly identical goals and values. All are utterly conscientious and strongly motivated to secure the survival of mankind and improve conditions in the future. That was the selection criterion. The result, an extreme variety of contrasting responses, was unexpected.

It is difficult to summarize the resources of a group with such extraordinary diversity.

Sperry, with a background world view of nature evolving through constant production and abandonment of dead ends and mistakes, warns of reliance on traditional science as well as traditional religion. He recommends a middle way that combines the critical, rational attitude of science with the ultimate goal of higher spiritual development promoted by religion. Concentrating on the phenomenon of emergence in nature and especially on the causative aspects of newly emerged entities, he REVISES not only religion, but also SCIENCE TO INCORPORATE CONSCIOUS EXPERIENCE, ideas, and ideals as major determining factors into a new view of the world. With that revision, science would in fact lose all its traditional disadvantages. An immensely fruitful perception of reality would take its place.

Konner's world combines love of humankind with a thorough understanding of its genetic heritage and bondage. It is his view that not rejection but understanding of the limitations of human nature will lead to the greatest unfolding of its possibilities. He is one of the rare males who recommends a STRONGER FEMALE INFLUENCE in politics and other public affairs—next to reduction of population increase and reduction of unlimited acquisition of material wealth. His demonstration of the benefit of admitting human limitations and using them as building blocks for psycho-social progress stands out among respondents, nearly all of whom consider human possibilities as "endless" or "unlimited." Boulding, with a background in economics, demands the combination of compassion with realism and warns of blind passion as the enemy of truth.

Tucker and Dunn speak from a religious and spiritual background and believe that we should accept differences as natural and promote unity in diversity. Others (e.g., Goble; Benson and Engeman; and Stein) concentrate on the moral revival within the United States. For them, the problem is not one of searching for the right values, but of implementing the values we already have.

In contrast, Chomsky and Herman concentrate on the evil perpetrated in the world through the values we consider untouchable. To act in our own interest, we protect foreign governments committing atrocities. There is no word about worse atrocities committed by our opponents (directly, not only at arm's length) from which it is our intent to protect the world—and therefore their literature might invite the accusation of bias. Nevertheless, most of the information is probably true and extremely thought-provoking. Their work, as well as that of Popkin, McMahan, and others lets the DANGER SIGNALS glow red hot. Can a country that protects evil be defended with a clear conscience? Can religious fundamentalism, which joyously expects a triumphant apocalypse, be trusted to prevent nuclear warfare? Is unilateral nuclear disarmament a rational suggestion at the present time?

De Kerckhove emphatically denies the latter. His love of the bomb—as a means of bringing humanity together—is the most unusual point of view expressed so far.

That radiation generated by nuclear war cannot under present circumstances extinguish the human race and that the total megatonnage of the world's stockpiles is declining seems to provide grounds for relief. —Yet undescribable damage would be done and democracy would not survive (Lackey, 1984).

It is hard to conceive that such a variety of contrasting recommendations were elicited by a single, identical goal: a tolerable future for mankind. —The background perceptions of reality of most contributors are unknown and can only be guessed from their suggestions. Their influence on decision-making, however, is undeniable. If perception of reality is of such importance, how can violent confrontations be avoided, even with the best intent and while pursuing identical goals?

Much can be said for tolerance of diversity, for the enrichment of our lives through different thoughts. But how can torture and injustice be tolerated? How can ideologies be tolerated which aim for world domination? How can tolerance of irresponsible, thoughtless depletion of non-renewable resources and the degradation of life through unlimited population increase be defended?

A major tragedy lies in the lethal power of ideas whose truth is questionable; much senseless killing might be prevented through objective, scientific inquiries. Could the effect of the great global leveller, science, be beneficial after all? Could its method of doubt and verification lead humanity onward to greater mental maturity? —Maybe it could, but only if the emptiness in its wake can be avoided; only if science is changed, to incorporate respect for the human soul into the world view it promotes.

A list of recommended values for the end of this chapter had been compiled and discarded. —The relevance of the present project lies in the arousal of thoughts about needed guidelines; in the motivations transmitted, in the values implicit in, but not directly expressed through, the statements of different authors; in the many related facts and ideas submitted; and in the meaningful contexts through which values have been described and illuminated. Clear evidence of their context-dependence is, in fact, the most striking result of the project.

If a further condensation of data is demanded, however, it may be helpful to approach them from a different angle. With a focus on year of first publication of references that are cited and recommended, it is possible to discern a slight, reluctant, and occasionally reversed trend over time, flowing from adherence to rigid dogmas toward increasing openness to new knowledge, experience, and insight. That trend is especially visible in the sectors of religion and of science, but also to a certain extent in that of technological progress. Hope for our future lies in the encouragement of that trend.

Returning to my list with that image of a flow from rigid absolutism toward assimilation of new insights, and incorporating the insight of value-interrelatedness, it becomes now possible to present the values suggested in a somewhat more meaningful way:

Mental maturity, *open-mindedness*, and *critical, independent thinking* permit the selection of the most relevant components from *intuition*, *reason*, *knowledge*, *experience*, *understanding*, and *insight*. They permit us to arrive at the *wisdom* we need to develop global consciousness and to include in our *love* and *compassion* the generations of the future and the world they will inherit. Such wisdom includes *policy restriction to pragmatic ground rules* which would lead in the *direction of greater humanity* without inhibiting its achievement through strangling the *free play of ingenuity and aspirations*. It suggests policies that would bring about *positive-sum results* and the application of the *co-evolutionary research ideology* to the products of human thought in general. It furthermore suggests *realism* and *responsibility*, which lead to respect for *decency*, *truth*, and *trustworthiness*, as the basis upon which our survival depends.

Like responsibility, *intelligence* and *tolerance* are "dependent" values; as components of wisdom they will elevate humanity, without deeper insight enlightened by love they may destroy it. The view that mankind does not deserve to survive has been expressed by highly intelligent persons. —Tolerance, if generalized unconditionally, will permit evil to spread. —Likewise, freedom, isolated from other values, is impossible and self-destructive; in combination with decency, responsibility, and respect for other persons, the biosphere, and conditions for coming generations, it is the most promising incentive for human ingenuity, the best guarantor for our happiness, and the most valid hope for our future. Another "dependent" value is *education*. Children and adults may be "educated" and conditioned to hate against their normal inclinations; to feel wants and desires far beyond those normally present. The former is a time-honored component of success in wars, the latter has become a sophisticated industry in the present. Most beneficial is education to think independently and critically. The benefit to mankind of a greater understanding of the human mind, similarly, depends upon the values of the persons who make use of that understanding; in general, however, any approach toward the truth will help us. One of the greatest truths in need of being rediscovered is probably that humanity cannot succeed without some kind of *higher guidance for human action*. Our future will depend upon the impact of *modern-day prophets* who have the wisdom to combine new knowledge with ancient insights.

Cooperation, *female participation in decision-making*, and *optimism* are the remaining values recommended. —Again, these are "dependent" values. Readiness to cooperate, based on the willingness to understand another person's point of view, is generally an asset. Extraordinary persons, however, may lead humanity forward just because they refuse to cooperate with superficiality and evil. The impact of females on decision-making is valuable only if they are *proud* of their differences from the male, of the special contributions they have to bestow on humanity, and *not* if they copy male aggressiveness and inflexibility and try to be "just like" males. Optimism, too, may be inappropriate if it leads to unrealistic expectations. If, however, as it does at the present, our fate depends on the discovery of, and the courage to pursue, a minuscule possibility to succeed against incredible odds, optimism may be the only attitude to help us.

The preceding treatment of values still leaves me dissatisfied; it is far too abstract. Taken out of context and collected into long lists, values become barren, dry, meaningless. They arise from, and come alive in, emotion-laden situations, and their meaning lies in the actions they induce; their expression in words is always defective.

For our most vital values, those born of emotions that determine the worth we assign to humanity, there are no words.

CONCLUSION AND RECOMMENDATIONS

Values are interrelated and context-dependent, except for key values like wisdom, mental maturity, open-mindedness, and well-informed concern for humankind, our earth and our future—together with constant vigilance and the readiness to shift course if unexpected and unforeseen obstacles appear in our way.

One of the most remarkable results of the project is, in fact, the insight it permits into the dependency of a value as widely promoted as intelligence. In isolation, intelligence can be "the most dangerous product of evolution"; combined with emotional sentiments, such as human warmth, intelligence becomes a component of wisdom and as such ascends to the very apex of our most urgent needs. —Similar dependency has been found for other highly regarded values.

A trend in time from rigid dogmatism to the acceptance of new insights can be discerned and is promoted. —Other insights which arose during the present research work—especially near its completion—are listed in the following section. It was observed that preoccupation with the project finally led to immediate and almost involuntary discernment and extraction, from unrelated reading material and from lectures, of factors important for humankind's future, and to the perception of their interrelationship. —If the question is one of broadening our perspective and of complementing our narrow and dangerous specialist world with capable generalists, research projects like the present one (preferably much larger and with the help of computers, reaching out into different countries and into different segments of the population) are therefore wholeheartedly recommended. They may provide one of the best ways to establish future-oriented global consciousness and to render nuclear weapons or other horrors superfluous.

The most important result of the project—made even more outstanding through its appearance already in a sample as small as the present one—is the discovery that, even if aims are identical, and even if values are identical, suggestions for actions to be taken may be vastly different, depending on a respondent's background and personal experiences. —Therefore, not values themselves, but the perception of reality from which they arise and through which they are interpreted and translated into action, must demand our main attention.

The question becomes: Is it possible to retain the diversity of thought which makes humanity unique and interesting, and yet to avoid the self-destruction of our species through the defence of incompatible rigid beliefs and passions?

Our major aim must become to progress further toward mental maturity, the first step toward wisdom (which includes knowledge in addition). If adherence to symbols and dogmas can be gently and carefully replaced by understanding of the *basic content* of one's own ideology, obstacles are removed from the understanding of the basic content of different ideologies. In all sectors of society, and in all parts of the world, progress from dogmatism to liberalism leads to a more secure future.

To achieve that progress, we have to rely on individuals gifted to facilitate that transition. As the present project reveals, such individuals exist in our society—and without doubt also in other ones. Their impact, however, is minimal—often in spite of life-long dedicated efforts—because it is overshadowed by the attitudes and products of money-oriented communication media committed to satisfy (and in the process to condition) a sensation-hungry majority. Conscientious, responsible, future-oriented work appealing to a selective audience is disregarded; vitally needed, irreplaceable gifts are lost.

It is therefore recommended that farsighted private persons raise foundations which assist in the selection and publication of valuable ideas and thoughts which would not sell well enough to make a profit for the publisher. (The pioneer work by Ruth Nanda Anshen is an example.)

It is recommended that schools and universities draw the attention of their students to such publications and that they be advertised to make them available to serious thinkers.

It is furthermore recommended that institutions be founded concerned with the generation of responsibility for our future (perhaps making use of projects similar to the present one) *and* with objective investigations of conflicting claims which arouse constant hostility. The adoption of the co-evolutionary research ideology responsible for the successes of science (a method which permits the illumination and revision of two opposing theories through new discoveries on either side) is strongly recommended to replace unyielding fanaticisms. Our future depends upon the replacement of erroneous beliefs—and their defence to the death—with agreement on undisputable facts. For such research to proceed without pressure from either the left or the right, reliance on mental maturity becomes even more essential.

The most urgent necessity, therefore, is the provision of a forum to those who would lead us toward greater mental maturity.

To give weight to my recommendations, I wish to repeat: We are responsible for the fate of our earth and the fate of future generations. We must therefore work toward the abolition of nuclear weapons. Such an abolition, however, may invite even greater dangers to mankind unless we can find universally acceptable values leading to conditions worthy of human beings. As the present project shows, the discovery and acceptance of such values is impeded through contrasting assumptions about basic aspects of reality. Top priority must therefore be given to values promoting closer approach to the truth.

INSIGHTS

We need open-mindedness to take full advantage of all mental resources humanity has to offer.

*

We need a new attitude in politics similar to the co-evolutionary research ideology which has greatly contributed to the success of science. That ideology encourages the approach of two opposing theories toward a common intermediate position closer to the truth than any of the former through a method in which successful research results in the pursuit of one of these theories elicit new insights, adjustments, and research designs in the opposing one. These, in turn, illuminate and adjust the former, and so on, until the best possible approach to the truth is reached. Often, none of the original theories has to be abolished, but each is enriched and enlightened by the opposing one.

An example is clash between the theory that poverty and slums cause diseases and the theory that diseases are caused by germs—two views which 100 years ago or more were fighting each other fanatically. We now know that poverty and slums cause diseases *because* germs proliferate under these conditions. There is no reason left why one of these theories should be defended *against* the other one.

If such methods could be applied to solve political and ideological disagreements, wars will become unnecessary and humanity will have made an immense step forward.

*

We need justice. But such justice is not provided by those who were treated with injustice; it is provided by those who treat other persons with justice and respect, whether or not their own experiences had been fortunate or unfortunate.

*

We need a larger perspective that lifts us from narrow, selfish concerns to the recognition that we are part of a web which includes our biosphere, and that damage to our biosphere will result in damage to our own nature, not only physically, but also —and most of all—mentally.

*

We need wisdom. The most serious waste of natural resources is the waste of intelligence in the service of the accumulation of material wealth.

*

We need peace. But peace cannot be achieved through relinquishment of weapons before sufficient mental maturity worldwide has been established to rely on contracts and just laws. Unilateral disarmament at the present time would not secure peace; it might increase hatred and cruelty through the silencing of voices of reason. Even dominance of a worldwide totalitarian regime would not bring peace, nor would it guarantee the survival of humanity. Through the ruthless combat of internal dissent and passionate reaction to it, more frightening and more easily hidden weapons, such as chemical or biological ones, might be developed. Peace can be achieved only through the promotion of mental maturity and wisdom.

*

We need values promoting reduction of unlimited population increase and reduction of unlimited increase of material wealth. Neither of them will be accepted, nor with good conscience can be promoted, in isolation. Without the reduction of both, life for the majority of human beings on earth will be seriously degraded.

*

We need flexibility, the readiness to change our convictions and actions if they turn out to lead to unintended, unanticipated, and undesirable consequences (T. E. Jones, 1980).

*

We need to understand the difference between absolute and relative poverty. Absolute poverty leaves human beings without a minimum of necessary food and shelter. It is degrading, and it is damaging to a person's health. Absolute poverty in a wealthy world is a crime which cannot be condoned and must never be allowed to exist.

Relative poverty, however, the state of possessing less than another person, can exist even if the poorer of the two is quite well-off and adequately supplied with food, shelter, health care, and even education. Relative poverty is largely a state of mind. If contempt from the outside and jealousy from the inside are absent, relative poverty need not interfere with happiness and bliss.

Promoters of complete equality should ponder the question whether, if it turns out that incentive to produce depends upon reward, it would not be better to have part of the population live in relative poverty than all of it in absolute poverty.

*

We need freedom. But the complexities of life in a large society are such that even the best functioning human nervous system is unable to handle them without the help of centuries of accumulated wisdom available to us in the form of values. Our nervous system is predisposed to accept, and act in accordance with, learned values—similar to the way it is predisposed to accept and learn languages. To mistake freedom for a license to live without values would be a fatal mistake; but we are free to question the values we have and to adjust them to take into account knowledge which was unavailable in ancient times. Human survival, in fact, depends upon the use we make of that freedom.

*

We need further advance toward the truth. We believe too many things that are not true. The greatest tragedy on earth is the sacrifice of valuable lives for wrong convictions.

*

We need concern for future generations. Any ethic or ideology without that concern endangers our species; with that concern, it confers a profound meaningfulness to life itself: It transforms mortal beings into immortal ones.

*

We need generalists. Evolution is marked by specialists in dead ends and generalists as the basis of spectacular advances. The evolution of ideas is no exception.

*

We need responsibility. Freedom will permit the fullest development of all potentials inherent in humanity, but the quality of these potentials is unknown. As a rudderless ship drifts into cliffs, so mankind will drift into disaster if irresponsible persons are permitted to limit the impact of responsible, future-oriented thinking.

*

We need penetrating insights which would speed up human mental evolution as dramatically as the work of enzymes speeds up organic metabolism.

*

We need a clear separation between high regard for decency and dignity on the one hand, and high regard for material wealth on the other. —The merging of the two by Hayek and similar thinkers is detrimental to the future quality of existence.

*

We need to develop a motivation other than short-sighted self-interest to secure sane and sensible productivity. The sacrifice of good ideas for *laissez-faire* egoism is as atrocious as the sacrifice of good ideas for rigid authoritarianism. There *are* responsible, committed, and farsighted persons on earth. Our fate depends upon their influence.

CHAPTER THIRTEEN

The Global Heart

In the July 1994 issue of Humankind Advancing, *Erdmann returned to one of the central themes of her doctoral dissertation, but this time likened the need for greater coordination among individuals and groups working for a better world to the way in which an embryo's cells begin to work together as the organism develops toward maturity. The piece is reprinted here with only minor edits to remove specific references to the other contents of that issue of the quarterly and allow it to stand on its own.*

The development of the heart of a bird, which can be observed by microscope using eggs at different stages of gestation, is a spectacle of unforgettable impact.

First, everything is quiet. Then, individual cells, dispersed randomly through the egg yolk, begin to twitch more or less violently. These twitching cells attract one another, larger groups of twitching entities appear, and, finally, all these cells are combined into one large vibrating clump—the future heart. But the heart is not functional at the outset. For several days the twitching remains uncoordinated, and the blood is pumped—sometimes slower and sometimes faster—back and forth in different directions in the adjacent blood vessels, which in the meantime have also developed. Then, finally, the heart "knows" what to do. The blood is pushed vigorously in only one direction. The heart is functional. The organism is alive!

Whenever I am reflecting on the small, uncoordinated groups and individuals, each with a different dream of how to achieve peace, harmony, and a sane future for humanity—often contradicting one another and working at cross-purposes, but with the same great vision of a unified whole—I cannot help being reminded of those biology labs where we observed the development of a heart. The difference, of course, is that the development of the heart occurs according to a blueprint laid down in the organism's surviving DNA after millions of unsuccessful attempts. Humanity's future evolution, on the other hand, has no such blueprint to guide it. Ours may be the first attempt to achieve such a larger whole—the first of millions, and destined to fail. On the other hand, we may succeed. Our great advantage is the evolution of consciousness, thought, and foresight—and of science.

The widely dispersed, unorganized, irregularly twitching heart cells are brought to their senses by chemoaffinity, a selective chemical attraction to one another (the discovery of which was Roger Sperry's first great contribution to neuroscience). What is the equivalent of chemoaffinity at the human level? What will bring us to our senses? —I believe that it is wisdom—the insight that neither science alone nor love for humanity alone will allow us to succeed, but that both are needed.

What is missing, however, is the grand design, the DNA blueprint, according to which embryonic development proceeds. That definite goal and aim is absent in evolution, unless it can be provided by visions at the highest level of consciousness. One of the most potent visions is the idea of God—the merging of infinite foresight, love, and knowledge.

The need for science has been expressed best and most succinctly by the philosopher Karl Popper: "On the pre-scientific level, we are often ourselves destroyed, eliminated with our false theories; we perish with our false theories. On the scientific level we systematically try to eliminate our false theories—we try to let our false theories die in our stead."

The need for science's complement—love for humanity—is vividly felt by each of the contributors to this quarterly, *Humankind Advancing*.

Let us always keep in mind the efforts of single, isolated individuals or small groups—often working at cross-purposes—and assist if we can their striving to find one another, to agree with one another, and in so doing to develop a functioning global heart.

CHAPTER FOURTEEN

A Dream Come True

Most of Erdmann's writings deal with the "big picture"—with global issues, the nature of consciousness, and the meaning of evolution. But however much one may be concerned with such things, life itself is lived one day at a time on a scale that is local, personal, and circumscribed in time and space. Erika wrote a number of essays that illuminated the links between the global and the personal, and it seems fitting to conclude Forging a Human Future *with several of them. For instance, a tragic change in her own life, and the unexpected events that followed, prompted this reflection on human nature, and what may be lost in our headlong rush into a wired and digitized future. "A Dream Come True" first appeared in* Humankind Advancing *in July 2001.*

It was a very sad occasion, the death of my dear husband, that led me to realize that, at least in some parts of the world, the dream that seems utterly utopian and impossible, the dream that all people will become one caring family, has actually been realized.

The winter was just beginning, and I was suddenly confronted with all kinds of new tasks and decisions that my husband had always dealt with, and about which I knew nothing. One of them was the removal of the snow banks that would block the long exit-way from our house to the road. We had a snow-blower I had no idea how to operate; besides, it was far too heavy for me to handle. I would have to pay someone to do it, but did not know how much and whether I had that money to hand. —But when I asked one of my neighbors for his suggestions, he immediately offered to do it for free. "That would just be a neighborly thing to do," he said, when I hesitated to accept his offer. I had been on friendly terms with all my neighbors, but preferred a life of solitude, without intimacy and friendly chatter, on our isolated point jutting out into the ocean. Thus I was unprepared for, and astonished by, their generosity.

—But the neighbor I had asked never had a chance to prove his helpfulness. Together with the first few inches of snow, another neighbor farther down the main road appeared with her car and drove back and forth to make a pathway for me to get to my mailbox. Not only that: from my window I saw her jumping out of the car with a snow shovel and clearing a path to my front door—all this on her way to go shopping in town and with her 6-year-old boy in the car.

The day proceeded, and the snow came down thick and heavy. But with it came a snow plow, fastened to the car of someone living still farther way and completely unknown to me. He cleared my driveway, turned, and disappeared—without waiting for compensation or even a word of thanks. I was utterly astonished. Only later did I hear from my children that people in the country do such things for one another.

I had heard about "New Age Community" groups for many years—how they started with high ideals, and how they invariably disintegrated after some time. Such ideals, I had concluded, were impossible in reality. –And now, here, I saw them recognized! —Later I had many more, even better experiences of neighborly helpfulness, and I am aware of the danger of taking them for granted. But I will never forget the deep impression these first fully unexpected instances had made.

"There is hope for our world," I thought—but then I realized that it was a world of the past, a world that is fast disappearing. Speed-intoxicated futurists disparagingly call these wonderful people "turtles," implying that there will be no room for them in the fast-track world of the future. –Yes, scientific progress and ingenious inventions have helped and are helping to eliminate much of human suffering and misery, and yet—without the "turtles"—the very heart of humanity would vanish.

CHAPTER FIFTEEN

The Need for Purpose and Meaning: Letter to a Neighbor

"Letter to a Neighbor" is something of a follow-up piece to "A Dream Come True." In various forms of art—haiku coming first to mind—profound meanings are best expressed with extreme economy. Much of Erdmann's work dealt with the need for humanity to find meaning and purpose in a new, scientifically informed view of the world that nonetheless respected the emotional resonances and traditions of our ancient faiths. The need for meaning is as important to human survival (whether of the individual or the species) as the need for air, food, or water, as Erika observed firsthand in the fall of 2002 and then wrote about, in this concise yet poignant essay.

Dear Warren,

Your house across the bay is still standing, but the light, reflecting its comforting beam in the water each evening, has gone out. You have left—forever.

When one of my neighbours called me earlier than usual in the morning to tell me that you were missing, I wasn't too concerned; you often went for long walks or bike rides alone. Only when a search helicopter flew over the bay and the surrounding area, sometimes nearly touching the roof of my house, did the seriousness of the situation sink in. Then an RCMP officer came and asked when I had seen you last. I felt guilty to admit that it may have been weeks or even months ago.

They found your suicide note around noon. "I cannot any more go on living like that. . . . Tell the RCMP to look for me on the Eastern Shore." (Even in the hour of your death you did not want anyone to waste time or money on you.) There, a short stretch away from the high shoreline cliffs, between the islands in front of my window, the search helicopter found your body floating in the water, and a Coast Guard rescue boat picked it up.

"If my brother had said all the good things about my character that Randall said about Warren," the minister at the funeral service declared, "I would be happy. Kind-hearted, considerate, caring, were just a few of the qualities he attributed to him." The same sentiments were expressed by everyone in the tightly packed little church. Everyone loved you. Why, then, could you not go on living? No terminal disease was involved, nor were you left abandoned because you were deaf when you lost your job as a fish-plant worker, not even when your mother died shortly afterward. A large and caring extended family looked after your needs, and you took part in all their celebrations. But in the middle of their joy, their laughing and joking, you were utterly alone within your wall of silence.

"It cannot be imagined how lonely a deaf person feels." This sentence, which I had read a few weeks ago, had led to another of my half-hearted attempts to fill your empty life with purpose. You had been the first person I had approached, after my husband's death in December 2000, with a request for snow shovelling during the winter, mentioning that I would pay you appropriately. You would be glad to do it, you said, and you would not want any pay. "That would be just a neighborly thing to do." Of course, I could not speak to you directly; you would not have understood me. My request, and your answer, were relayed by your sister-in-law. Only a very few of your closest relatives or steady companions since early childhood knew how to get through to you, with gestures they had invented, or with certain positions of their mouths and lips. You never had any formal training in sign language or lip reading, nor had they. Our place is much too isolated for such services; and to send you away to live with strangers somewhere seemed the worst punishment.

As the winter of 2001 proceeded, so many other neighbors and friends of mine had volunteered for snow shovelling that you were not needed. In summer, it was the same with lawn mowing, tree cutting, or diverse odd jobs. You were not needed. "Don't bother Warren," they told me each time, "he can't understand you. I will do it." And your life remained empty and without purpose. I felt vaguely uneasy about this, but not enough. In fact, I was quite glad about all the generous help I received. "One day," I thought, "they will get tired of helping me, then I'll find a way to get through to you (with a bit of assistance) and, once grasped, the tasks you could do for me would become something you would look forward to." —That day never came.

"He must have been very depressed," a relative told me—and then, when I related my plans, she added, "He would have done everything for you—and he wouldn't have wanted any money for it."

I now know, Warren, why you could not live like that any longer. You died of an empty life—a life without meaning and purpose.

Had I known how much you suffered—

Had you known how often you were on my mind—

But for all this it is now too late.

Your neighbor, Erika

CHAPTER SIXTEEN

Roger Sperry: A Personal View

Erdmann spent more than a decade working with Roger Sperry, an experience she found profoundly exciting and stimulating. While our book Beyond a World Divided *was primarily concerned with Sperry's scientific work and his ideas about the nature of consciousness, Erika also wanted to speak, if only briefly, not just of Sperry-the-scientist but of Sperry-the-human-being. Our editor suggested including her thoughts as an epilogue to the book. It is, I think, an evocative portrait of one of the great scientific figures of the mid-twentieth century.*

from BEYOND A WORLD DIVIDED (1991)

And now, in the end, I should be less abstract and say something concrete about the person whose philosophy I have discussed. This is difficult for me. If I think about him in concrete terms at all—and this is rare because the significance of his work for our future predominates—I see a lover of solitude, of nature, of beauty, of poetry. I see a striver for excellence, incessantly dissatisfied with himself and with others. I see everything he touches, even the products of his spare time, turn into masterpieces. The sculptures he made turn his home into a museum of exquisite taste. His interest in fossils led to his discovery of one of the largest ammonites in the world, now mounted at one end of the living room. But he is not easy to live with, and his wonderful wife has been called a saint.

I see a perfectionist, a disciplined laborer, improving his own writing through innumerable revisions and demanding the utmost of himself with an obsession bordering on cruelty. But he does not work constantly; his "anti-brain-strain activities" (his own expression)—carefully scheduled to achieve top performance during working hours—include relaxed evenings at home and weeks of fishing, swimming, or exploring the remote and barren shorelines of the Baja, a rocky Mexican peninsula jutting into the Pacific.

If an urgent task demands it, however, he is a tremendous worker. At the age of 72, ravaged by his slowly progressing paralysis, he rewrote a long and difficult paper—a job I estimated would take several months—within a single week, *although he had to undergo an eye operation during that same week.*

The three words describing his nature most accurately would be *courage*, *willpower*, and *self-discipline*. Most of all, I see him as a fighter—drawn by difficulties, conquering obstacles anyone else would judge undefeatable.

This is the man who has set himself the task of turning the world of Arnold's "Dover Beach"—the world with "neither joy nor love nor light"—into a much more real one, a world in which joy and love and light are part of the reality of scientists as well as of the religious; a world in which we may hope again, like the pioneers of the Enlightenment, that the "clash of ignorant armies at night" may be ended in the coming of a new dawn.

But how can Sperry's point of view be integrated into the solid, broader framework of human knowledge? How can the merging of science and values become a self-evident part of the majority's mind-set?

Someone who worked closely with Sperry for over 30 years once said: "Dr. Sperry is such a genius; if he just knew how to acknowledge the work of others, the world would lie at his feet."

Another person, himself one of the greatest scientists I know, seemed to have more insight. "I can understand him," he said of Sperry; "his thoughts are too valuable, his time is too valuable. He cannot be expected to penetrate into the minds of others and even less to adjust the expression of his own ideas to the framework of their conceptions. We have to do that for him."

Echoes from these two conversations follow me everywhere: "The world would lie at his feet" and "We have to do that for him."

CHAPTER SEVENTEEN

Letter to a Sister

Much is written these days about the links between "the personal and the political," or, more broadly, about the differences between how we act in our private lives and the values and views we proclaim publicly. Erika was more successful than most at harmonizing these two aspects of her life and living the values she espoused. Yet even she was not always able to avoid disagreements about such matters with those closest to her, or to convince them of the correctness of her point of view. Over the nearly 30 years that I knew her, it struck me that a certain kind of tolerance lay at the heart of Erika's worldview: an understanding that reasonable people might not always agree, that there was often more than one "right" way to look at a situation, and that sometimes there were very good reasons why people held convictions that might seem outdated or, in the light of the latest scientific research, just plain wrong. I see evidence of that tolerance in the following essay, which originally appeared in Humankind Advancing. *You can't read it without thinking that Erika was convinced that it was her way of thinking that was correct. Yet the other side of the argument is presented fairly, and in the end one concludes that, right though Erika may be, her perspective does not come without emotional and, indeed, personal cost. There may be answers, but not easy ones. Thus it seems fitting to close the book with this moving reflection.*

Dear Ursula,

Nearly three years have gone by since you passed away. Your last letter to me, written a few weeks before your death, has been left unanswered; you had harshly criticized my Ph.D. thesis, "In Search of Values for Human Survival," and I was struggling for words that would not hurt you. Before I could find them, we were separated forever.

To you, the very idea that the survival of humankind could be in question appeared absurd. Likewise, you were appalled by the thought that our traditional values might be insufficient to handle our immense present problems, and that shifts in value priorities might be needed. "Values," you wrote, "should not shift their priorities; they should be solid as the earth itself." The vast majority will share your conviction; yet how can we ignore the enormous increase in knowledge that has taught us about cause-effect relationships we never suspected? How can we ignore a globe shrinking in relation to its population? —The earth and its bounty were endless for billions of years; they are so no more, and we are forced to ask questions that have never before been asked.

Further, you thought it would be harmful to students to be introduced to the seriousness of our problems. "They would lose their faith in mankind and even regret that they and their parents are part of it." —But everything I write, I think, I say, is determined by the wish that such despair might be avoided! You accuse me of bringing about dangers by talking of their possibility. The opposite is true. As death, and our knowledge of it, increases the worth of life, so knowledge about the danger to our species and our earth will open our eyes to their unique and marvelous promises.

You believed that my concerns are senseless because improvements will occur "in an evolutionary way." —But are not human concerns and efforts part of this process?

As an artist, you deplored the fact that my questionnaire, going to ten different sectors of our society—religious persons, scientists, the mass media, and so on—had bypassed artists. "Why didn't you ask any artists?" you wrote. "They have a tremendous influence on people. Think of all the beautiful melodies written over hundreds of years [that] still make people cry with joy. (But then you probably don't agree with my belief that people need to be happy, need to have hope, and need to have faith in order to find purpose in life.)"

How could you have thought of me like that! Of course, I believe that people need to be happy and have hope and faith to find purpose in life—though faith must be founded in one's intent, one's will, and one's abilities, not in someone or something else. And I believe that artists have a vital role to play in the survival of our species. Without their contributions, life would lose its meaning. I even believe that they should not feel obliged to dampen their creativity and worry about our future instead (and so I did not send my questionnaire to them)—but they *should* respect the thinkers and doers who do face reality courageously and who work to prevent foreseeable dangers.

And yet, there is so much in your letter with which I fully agree. "With everything I do, I think of not messing up our great beautiful earth," you wrote—and then you described your lifestyle, a far more conscientious one than I lead, for which I admire you. —You speak of the values to live by as "*education*, involving also *simplicity*, *honesty*, *mind-opening*, *preserving nature*, and *preventing waste*." You also believe, as I do, that love and compassion are part of human nature and—with few exceptions—will surface as the need arises.

Yet you seem to forget that these "few exceptions" can have an impact—for good or evil—that is out of proportion to their numbers. And you leave out two values of such high priority that our entire future depends upon them: *thoughtfulness* and *responsibility*. Without these, even love can be destructive.

There is poetry in your writing and thinking. "The people in India," you say, "are happy to be poor, because this way they feel closer to God. They believe: If you walk through a forest which is owned by you, your thoughts are troubled with worries about diseases of trees, the value of the wood, the damage caused by animals, etc. But if you walk through a forest owned only by nature, your thoughts are elevated by its beauty."

I have read of a different India, however. Günter Grass (who was there) reports "rats scurrying underfoot, crows and vultures flapping close overhead; hundreds of children gathering sticks and breaking off branches for firewood—which is why the forests are dying, why nothing grows again except children. Families, pavement dwellers they are called, sleep on sidewalks, along walls, each sleeping a different sleep. Young men sit on their haunches, in their faces the resigned anxiety, the concentrated gravity of those who no longer have anything to wait for. People are starving, dying in apathy."

My God, what did I do! I did not want to worry you—and I must find consolation in the fact that you cannot read these lines. Yet I cannot leave them unwritten. They are part of the truth we most urgently need. Grass describes a situation that will spread over the entire globe unless we face it honestly and struggle hard to prevent it.

You would not approve. "I believe," you write, "how hard people struggle is not really important. The Universe is unfolding as it should. . . . Population growth will be controlled—the question of waste will be answered and new resources will be found to feed them all."

And there are two paragraphs near the end—you must have written them only about three weeks before your death—which moved me most deeply.

"Sometimes I get the impression (I got it before you started to write about human values) that something very valuable and magnificent is missing in your thinking system: the joy of being alive! This you cannot acquire through books, talks or other people's thoughts. This you can only feel. Close your eyes and listen to the powerful or lovely tunes of our best composers (Wagner, Mozart, Beethoven, Verdi, Strauss, just to name a few) or listen to the beautiful singing voice of Luciano Pavarotti. There is an enormous swinging beauty hovering in the air which has more value than all the words and thoughts combined.

"There are millions of people with a joy of the world so deeply rooted, that even your fear-fed danger signals cannot reach them. It would be sad if you decided to spend the rest of your precious life with complicated thoughts of how to make the world better—and have no time to see and feel what a beautiful world it is."

I did not succeed in finding words to tell you that it is because I love the world so much I cannot close my eyes to the dangers that threaten it. *Because* I want millions of other persons—now and in the future—to share your joy in life, I have to contribute to our destiny to the best of my ability and in accordance with my nature. I wanted to transmit to you the profound feeling of happiness one can experience while working productively in the service of a self-chosen worthwhile goal.

Would you have understood?

Love, Erika

Bibliographic Note

Erika Erdmann published five book-length works during her lifetime, all of which are (to varying degrees) still available to interested readers:

1. *Realism and Human Values.* New York: Vantage Press, 1978. Her original self-published book on science and human values that led to Roger Sperry's inviting her to join him at Caltech as his library assistant.

2. *In Search of Values for Human Survival.* Ann Arbor, Mich.: University Microfilms International, 1987. Her doctoral dissertation.

3. *Challenge to Humanity: Values for Survival and Progress.* Dundas, Ont.: Peace Research Institute—Dundas, 1989. The condensed version of her doctoral dissertation, published as a combined "double number" of the serial *Peace Research Reviews.*

4. *Beyond a World Divided: Human Values in the Brain-Mind Science of Roger Sperry.* Co-authored with David Stover. Boston: Shambhala, 1991. Reprint: San Jose, Calif.: Author's Choice Press, 2000. This account of Sperry's work on the mind-brain problem is aimed at the general reader. A précis of Sperry's earlier scientific work is included, as well as a list of his key papers. The paperback edition from Author's Choice Press remains in print.

5. *A Mind for Tomorrow: Facts, Values, and the Future.* Co-authored with David Stover, Westport, Conn.: Praeger, 2000. In this follow-up to *Beyond a World Divided*, Erdmann and I attempted to put Sperry's views in the broader context of current world problems, and also drew links between his work on values and the broader humanist tradition. The book remains in print, and has also been made available as an ebook.

Editor's Notes

The purpose of this book is to make Erika Erdmann's works available to a new generation of readers. In order to do so most effectively, I have followed some general guidelines in relation to both the inclusion of references and the actual editing of the text.

Both *Realism and Human Values* and *Beyond a World Divided* included extensive endnotes and references when they first appeared, as did Erdmann's doctoral dissertation. In the excerpts from those works presented here, I have omitted those notes for the sake of ease of reading. Readers who would like to pursue the ideas presented are referred to the original texts, all of which are available either for purchase—new or used—through the usual roster of online stores, or through one's local library by means of interlibrary loan.

For those chapters which originally appeared as academic papers or articles, I have retained the references here, on the assumption that the original sources are in these cases less easily accessed.

Insofar as editing is concerned, I have tried to follow the guiding principle of minimalism, leaving Erika's unique (and powerful) voice unaltered. That said, there are a few sentences here and there, especially in the excerpts from *Realism and Human Values*, a book which was only lightly edited (if edited at all) before publication, which, it seemed to me, would benefit from being made clearer, and I have taken the copyeditor's liberty of doing so. In no cases have I altered the meaning of what Erika was trying to convey. The usual author–editor relationship allows the author the last word in reviewing her editor's suggested changes; obviously that course of action is impossible in this case, but Erika and I worked together long enough that I can at least hope that, in those few cases where I have made editorial changes, I have improved the text's readability in a fashion of which she would have approved.

Because this is a book meant to be read, not some sort of scholarly edition, I have silently corrected typographical errors in the original sources. Where substantive material has been omitted mid-passage, I have indicated that by means of an ellipsis, but if changes to capitalization or punctuation were required, I have simply gone ahead and done so without making use of the scholarly but, from the general reader's perspective, intrusive convention of including the interpolated characters in square brackets (e.g., "[A]nd"). For scholarly purposes, the original publications should be considered the "documents of record," and it is my hope that at least some readers, intrigued by what they read here, will seek out the original books and articles from which I have drawn.

Index

NOTE: Only Erdmann's own books are indexed by title. In the case of thematic entries, only substantive discussions are indexed. The preface and the bibliographic and editors' notes have not been indexed; nor have endnotes in those chapters containing them.

About the Author

Erika Erdmann was born in Germany on 16 January 1919. Her father, Edmund Altenkirch, was an internationally known scientist whose work in thermodynamics resulted in important advances in the areas of heating and refrigeration technologies, including research that contributed to the development of the heat pump. Erdmann credited her father for instilling in her a thorough understanding of the scientific method and an equally deep love for humanity. To avoid her being exposed to Nazi propaganda that was disseminated through the educational system, Erdmann was schooled at home for part of her childhood, and also assisted her father in his research until her marriage to Karl Erdmann in 1942.

In 1953 she and her husband emigrated to Canada, where he worked as an engineer for Domtar and they raised their four children. She enrolled in Sir George Williams University (now Concordia University) in Montreal in 1967 as a mature student, graduating with distinction in 1971. She went on to work as a research assistant for physiological psychologist Roy A. Wise, and with Wise published a paper, "Emotionality, Hunger, and Normal Eating: Implications for Interpretation of Electrically Induced Behavior," in the April 1973 issue of *Behavioral Biology*.

When her husband retired in 1972, they moved to Nova Scotia, where Erdmann worked for the local public library branch, and where she wrote her first book, *Realism and Human Values*. She started graduate work at Dalhousie University in 1981, concentrating on the relationship between science and human values, especially the work of Roger W. Sperry and Ralph Burhoe. From 1982 to 1990 she served as library research assistant for Roger Sperry at the California Institute of Technology; during that time she also completed her master's and doctoral degrees, and published *Beyond a World Divided*. In 1989 she founded the quarterly journal *Humankind Advancing*, and in 2000 published a second book on Sperry's work, *A Mind for Tomorrow*.

Erdmann continued to live and work in Lockeport, Nova Scotia, following the death of her husband Karl, until her own death in 2006.

www.ingramcontent.com/pod-product-compliance
Lightning Source LLC
LaVergne TN
LVHW091153080426
835509LV00006B/662

* 9 7 8 0 9 8 8 1 2 9 3 0 6 *